Speak Up & Get Out!

How to Survive & Thrive after the Devastation of Domestic Abuse & Violence

Dr. Tamika Anderson

ISBN: 978-1522810803

Table of Contents

Dedication v
Acknowledgements vii
Introduction 1

Chapter 1 – Overview 13
Chapter 2 – What is Abuse? The Turmoil Beneath the Water 23
Chapter 3 – Warning Signs: Is That Right? Did He Really Do That? . . . 67
Chapter 4 – Save Yourself 101
Chapter 5 – Prepare, Plan, and Protect 119
Chapter 6 – Enforce Boundaries 133
Chapter 7 – Ask Questions 149
Chapter 8 – Keep Your Information Safe 155
Chapter 9 – Making the Transition:
  Did I Do the Right Thing? Maybe I Shouldn't Have Left 161
Chapter 10 Now That You're On Your Own, Breathe,
  Grieve, & Be Good to Yourself 177
Chapter 11 – Thrive and Fly 203
Chapter 12 – Closing Thoughts 211

About the Author 217
Connect With Me! 218
Resources 219

Dedication

This book is lovingly dedicated to the women who are courageously surviving or survived domestic violence and abuse. I also dedicate this book to the thousands of women who have lost their lives in the fight to survive domestic violence and abuse.

Acknowledgements

First and foremost I would like to thank God. In the process of writing this book and reflecting on life, I am grateful for the gift of grace. On this journey I found the strength to turn my pain into power.

To my daughter, thank you for your love, your bravery, and for being such a courageous young woman.

To my Editor, thank you for not hesitating to work on such a controversial topic. David Ulery, you are much appreciated.

To *Some Place Safe*, I want to thank each one of you for your love and support. I thank you for treating me like a human being. I came to you broken into pieces, but you gave me comfort in knowing that I could put myself back together again.

Last but definitely not least, I also want to thank all of the Supporters of the Speak Up & Get Out Movement.

Introduction

> *"I have come to accept the feeling of not knowing where I am going. And I have trained myself to love it. Because it is only when we are suspended in mid-air with no landing in sight, that we force our wings to unravel and alas begin our flight. And as we fly, we still may not know where we are going to. But the miracle is in the unfolding of the wings. You may not know where you're going, but you know that so long as you spread your wings, the winds will carry you."* – C. Joy Bell C.

You are someone who believes you don't need this book. You have a wonderful marriage. You love your spouse. He loves you. He would never hurt you.

You may be in a strong marriage or a committed relationship. You may even be with someone who says he loves you forever. He has told you that you are his soul mate. Your abuser has convinced you that you are the only woman he has ever loved or wanted to marry.

He showers you with attention, gifts, poetry, and the most AH-mazing sex ever. He tells you there is no one else he would ever want to be with because no other woman understands him like you do. He cries for less than 30 seconds to tell you how heartbroken he's been from the way all of his exes cheated on him in the past and hurt him. Beware! This is a trap!

You immediately begin trying to prove to him that you're nothing like those other women. You want to prove your love and loyalty to him. You also don't want him to be in pain. Because you're a nurturing, kind and caring person, you want to "fix" him and make him feel better. You just can't understand why a woman would mistreat such a gentle, loving, caring, and attentive guy. After all, you think to yourself, he loves his mother. A man who loves his mother would have to treat his girlfriend or wife like a queen. WRONG!

Something doesn't sit right. You feel uneasy. Something's not right, but you're not sure what. You don't know who to talk to, or if you're just crazy. You don't want to talk to anybody, because you don't want to make him look bad. And you don't want to look like you're "too sensitive" or "crazy."

You've been told, "This is how we operate."

"This is how families operate."

"You feel like you are on an island by yourself because that is where you want to be."

Over time you discover the more you love him and the more you try to let him know you are nothing like the other women who hurt him in the past, something changes. You realize you have lost yourself in the process.

Or perhaps you've been abused by your spouse, your own mother, in laws, or other family members. You feel confused, lost, abandoned, rejected, and alone. Something tells you what's being done isn't right. When you finally reach out for help from family, friends, or clergy, you discover you've been slandered and talked about behind your back to these people. You find out they have been talking about you as if you have been mistreating the abuser.

What your family, friends, church members, and clergy don't know is that he's not the same person behind closed doors as he is in public.

He is so nice in public, people say,

"How could this deep dimpled face guy be verbally, emotionally, financially, spiritually, and physically abusive?"

"He is so funny and like a big cuddly teddy bear?"

"He is such a committed family man, why would he cheat with other women?"

You feel trapped. When you confide in someone about the things that are happening to you it sounds outrageous because they've never seen the dark side of your abuser. To add insult to injury, you have already been discredited to others by your abuser. So when you finally *say* something it seems so outrageous that these people may even laugh at you. They may even accuse you of being sensitive, exaggerating the situation, or trying to get attention.

As a result, you may fear speaking up about what's happening to you. Why?

For fear of not being believed,

For fear of someone betraying your confidence,

For fear of your life changing,

For fear of the future,

For fear of being punished by your abuser, and

For fear of being on your own.

I'm here to tell you, you're right. There *is* something wrong. You are not alone.

In this book, I will show you how to:

Recognize the warning signs and red flags

Avoid the mistakes

Create a safe exit strategy plan

Forgive your abuser

Forgive yourself

Not just survive but thrive after the devastation of domestic abuse and violence.

We will also explore how you can protect yourself and how to avoid the pitfalls of further abuse through the court system. If you're in denial like I was, your mother, grandmother, aunt, or friend bought this book for you.

Let's look at some of the warning signs. Is he very charming and attentive? Does he want all of your time? Yes, it feels good at first but now you are feeling somewhat smothered.

Did you used to come first all of the time, and now you find yourself playing second or third fiddle? Is he very secretive? You have poured your deepest secrets out to him. He has only shared superficial intimate details like how hurt he was when he lost his dog or the necklace his grandmother gave him. You know some material item or something superficial.

If you know you're in trouble, I am going to share some suggestions on how to get out. I will show you exactly what you need to do to protect yourself and your children. Once someone verbally, emotionally, or financially abuses you or doesn't respect your boundaries, this is a warning. This behavior is just the appetizer to their main course of physical abuse.

When the physical abuse starts, it does not stop no matter how badly you *want* it to stop. No matter how hard you try to make it better, it will only get worse. Physical abuse is the second to last stop of death on the train wreck of domestic violence. It's so important to Speak Up & Get Out while you still have the precious gift of life.

The more I tried to make my relationship better, the more my abuser laughed and treated me worse. He would even go as far as to tell me everything I did was wrong and that I never do anything right. I thought I knew what abuse was. It was not until I was physically abused to the point of almost losing my life that I began to understand. I suddenly realized I had been abused the entire 20 years of our relationship.

In this book you'll discover the different types of abuse, warning signs, personality types and characteristics of abusers, and the dangers of dating or marrying a mama's boy.

We're frequently told to leave a dangerous situation . We aren't told that leaving is just the beginning. We each will experience deep pain as we start to follow the path to healing. I will show you how to make the transition to begin your journey of healing emotionally and mentally. This step is so important. If you decide to leave you will experience guilt, shame, and even question whether or not you did the right thing. I'll help you understand why it's so hard to let go of a toxic relationship. Once you've made the transition you'll feel free to breathe, grieve, and be good to yourself. You will be on your path to survive and thrive.

As you read my story, always keep these things in mind. What you've gone through or what you're still going through is not your fault. You haven't done anything to deserve being used and abused. You can't change your abuser. You can't stop him from abusing you.

You can't love him enough to "fix" him, to ease the pain of his past or emotional trauma. Only he can make the non-negotiable decision to stop being abusive to you. Only he can decide that he will make the necessary changes to grow spiritually, emotionally, mentally, and personally. No matter what kind of emotional baggage he's carrying or internal garbage he dumps on you; he doesn't have an excuse to abuse you.

I know because I was there. I was in a verbally, emotionally, physically, financially, spiritually, and narcissistic abusive relationship for 20 years with my husband.

The last time my husband put a knife to my throat, a police officer took me to the side and said, "Look here, unless you make a change, the next time we come to your home it will be to take you out of here in a body bag." He continued to point at an umbrella on the floor and explained to me that my husband cared more about that umbrella on the floor than he cared about me.

I was confused, hurt, and embarrassed. I just didn't know how my life had changed so drastically in a split second. I couldn't comprehend how someone who claimed to have loved me so much could hurt me so deeply.

I had hand prints on my neck, blood on my shirt, and was visibly beaten up. Still, I told the police officer nothing happened because I didn't want my husband to go to jail. I especially didn't want him to go to jail with his colostomy bag. He had already been through enough with the horrible surgeries. I just wanted the pre-surgery husband back. I no longer knew this post-surgery life-threatening violent and angry husband. Even though I no longer knew him, I still tried to fix and save him without any concern for my own well-being.

Not just a Gladiator but a Survivor turned Thriver

Like many of you, I have had some ups and downs, some hurts and pains, trials and tribulations. There were times when I just couldn't see beyond the moment because I was so broken. I felt shattered into so many pieces that I didn't think I could ever be put back together. Even so, I'm still standing. The past few years from 2012 through 2015 have been the most painful. I'm still coming out of the firestorm. Even though this has been about the most excruciatingly painful time that I've ever experienced, I still manage to hold on. No one could have ever convinced me that this pain could be such a painful pain, so intense, or even exist for that matter.

The experience that I had shook me to my core. I didn't see it coming. I was completely blindsided by it. Like so many women, I blamed myself.

I felt like I wasn't enough or even good enough.

I felt like I wasn't worth it.

I felt like I had come face to face with a knife wielding Mike Tyson knockout that luckily "didn't use a closed fist" yet had the rage and force of an angry charging bull. I look back now and think if I would have pulled a Solange I wouldn't be here sharing my story with you today because he definitely showed me he was not a Jay-Z, he was more like Ike Turner who stopped just Short of O.J, and mirrored Columbus.

Who would have thought a situation like this would've later transformed me into not just a Gladiator but a Survivor who is now thriving. My situation made me say to myself in my best Tina Turner voice, "What's love got to do with it?"

I was so dazed and confused. I couldn't understand how my "protector" could physically turn on me in an instant just because he was angry about his own life experiences, circumstances, and shortcomings. In my state of confusion, I felt shame and guilt because it happened in front of our daughter. I tried so hard to be a good role model for her. I thought, "Wow, if I stay she'll think this is okay and will grow up to not know her own worth and how valuable she is as a woman.

I carried shame because the neighbors saw the policemen at our home too many times. One time was too many. I felt hurt because I couldn't understand. How could someone I loved so much and was so faithful and committed to could inflict such violent physical and emotional pain in the blink of an eye.

If you're out there and in a toxic relationship, I urge you to Speak UP. You may not even know you're in a toxic relationship that can lead to physical abuse. Abuse isn't always overt. I was being abused for 20 years in my relationship and I didn't know I was being abused until my abuser began to physically abuse me.

As we'll review later, abuse comes in many forms verbal, emotional, sexual, financial, spiritual, and physical. I'm going to share my personal story and experiences with you. Some people may think it is too revealing. I think it is important to be authentic, transparent and not give you fluff. It may save your life. If you believe you are experiencing abuse, contact your local domestic violence women's shelter for information, resources, and support. Another option is to work with a professional therapist who specializes in domestic abuse and violence.

Family and friends may or may not be supportive. Some of them may have good intentions, but because they're not professionally trained to deal with these situations, their well intended help could cost you your safety or even your life.

You may also learn that they don't want to get involved for various reasons or they just don't know how to help. Family members and friends often don't see the abuser as abusive because he's very nice, friendly, and charming in public to other people. I can't stress enough the importance of contacting the National Domestic Violence Hotline at 1-800-799-SAFE (7233) or your local women's shelter to speak with a trained professional who can help you.

I have a Doctor of Science in Information Systems & Communications, Master of Science in Organizational Leadership, and Bachelor of Arts in Psychology. I am also a Certified Financial Manager with the Department of Defense. I have over 15 years of combined Corporate and Government Service. I have also taught undergraduate and graduate university students in academia. I also coach, mentor, and speak to women nationally and internationally on how to escape domestic violence situations and help them heal from the pain of their past experiences, toxic relationships with people, and their relationship with money.

Because of my own experience, I developed my life-saving SPEAK Formula for this book, and I also developed the TALK formula that I have shared on NBC, FOX, ABC, and other major television networks. I want to share with you my mistakes, pitfalls, and valuable information I learned along the way.

I was clueless when it came to understanding domestic violence. I didn't know there were so many layers and contributing factors for the causes of domestic violence. No one could have ever convinced me that my husband would someday become violent towards me. When he started physically abusing me in a life-threatening manning is when I truly understood that I was being abused. However, I was still in denial. How could this deep dimpled face charming lovable guy turn so mean, cold, and physically abusive towards me? I initially didn't tell anyone about how he would call me names, lie, cheat, steal, manipulate, and play other people against me, play me against other people, and force me to do things I didn't want to do.

When I connected with my local women's shelter and began to share what I had endured over the years, I began to understand that I had been abused for much longer than when the physical abuse began because abuse is not just physical.

I also learned the term "gaslighting" from the prosecutor. I explained to her that since my husband was no longer in our home I was not misplacing my postage stamps, keys, or mail. The prosecutor said, "That's because he's been gaslighting you." Gaslighting is a tactic abusers use to confuse you and make you question yourself, and as a result it gradually lowers your self-esteem. It makes you question yourself and decreases your confidence. Gaslighting erodes your ability to trust your own decisions causing you to rely on your abuser for validation and permission to do things you feel you are no longer capable of doing or accomplishing. I had so many things happen to me over the years but, I never knew what I was experiencing had a name.

I'll share the terms with you as well as examples of from my personal experience. You will learn terms such as love-bombing, idealization, devaluing, discarding, smear campaign, flying monkeys, and many more…

You may already be familiar with these terms and if you're not familiar with the terms, if you are in an abusive relationship you will definitely be able to match your experience and the type of abuse you endure with your spouse or partner. Abusers also use a tactic called "word salad". It's a conversation or argument started by the abuser to keep you confused with accusations, questions you can't answer. You end up not knowing what the point of the conversation is or why you are having the discussion. This causes you to second guess yourself, doubt yourself, and ultimately lowers your self-confidence.

I thought he would change. I thought he'd realize that what he was doing was wrong and he would stop. I protected him, I didn't call the police, and I didn't go to the hospital to get an examination for my wounds to be treated. When the police came to our home, I would make excuses for him so he wouldn't be arrested and I covered for him.

He bullied me into not going to the hospital because he told me I better lie about how I got hurt. I didn't want to lie so I opted not to go to the hospital each time. He later laughed about how he didn't go to jail. He mocked me by recounting how I would scream and beg for him to stop beating me. He would tell me how beating me made him feel powerful and how he felt like a man. He also said he would beat me because he was afraid of losing me.

I tried so hard throughout my life to not become various statistics. I tried to explain to him that because he started beating me I am now a statistic of 1 in 4 women who are physically abused by a spouse or partner. He looked me in the eyes and laughed and said, "Oh so now you're a battered woman. You're a victim? You've labeled yourself."

"So what does that make me Tamika?" Does it make me an abuser? Huh?" He began to stomp towards me. When he saw me shake he began to laugh. He said, "You just got a few of the neighbor women an ass whooping. Their husbands are telling them right now that they better not call the police. Anyways, you are not a battered woman. I don't whoop your ass every day. There are women out there who would laugh at you or want to whoop *your* ass for saying you are a battered woman. They're getting their ass whooped every day. I don't throw you a beating every day. The last time I just tossed you around and slammed you. Besides, I don't hit you with a closed fist."

I became desperate for answers and I sought help from a therapist who introduced me to the terms narcissist and narcissism in a way I had never heard it used before and how it relates to narcissistic abuse. I always thought of a narcissist as someone obsessed with their looks or the classic image always came to mind of the man Narcissus staring at his reflection in the water. I was still confused, yet deeply saddened to learn I had been duped. I was charmed, valued, and I thought loved beyond measure by him only to find out that it was all a lie. The moment I began to set boundaries and no longer went along with everything he said is when I became enemy number one in his mind.

The SPEAK Formula

As a result of my experience I developed the SPEAK Formula to help other women like myself. I highly encourage you to use my SPEAK Formula because the high level of danger you're exposed to with your abuser can be deadly.

When you are being verbally or emotionally abused, you must have a safety plan because this abuse is a prelude to physical abuse that can be deadly. My SPEAK formula will prepare you ahead of time, so you will know what to do in an emergency. If you think, "If I just do exactly what he says, he won't abuse me." Think again. Create your own plan with the information provided in the SPEAK Formula and know your safety plan.

S stands for Save Yourself from your abuser.

Take the necessary actions to make sure you and your children are safe.

P stands for Prepare and Protect yourself physically, financially, legally etc…

E stands for Enforce boundaries you create.

Abusers hate boundaries so it is very important to create them and enforce those boundaries for your safety.

A stands for Ask questions.

Get on the phone and contact the National Domestic Violence Hotline at 1-800-799-SAFE (7233) or a trained professional therapist that specializes in working with women of domestic violence and abuse. If you are in immediate danger please call 911.

K stands for Keep your information safe.

Place all of your important documents in a large envelope or box safely hidden from your abuser.

You will learn how to implement my life saving SPEAK Formula. You will also grow mentally and emotionally which will help you rebuild your self-esteem, self- worth, and regain your personal freedom. You will know exactly what to do and how to do it.

I will give you step-by-step tools and strategies you can implement immediately to get results. The goal is to rebuild your self-confidence to know you can accomplish tasks on your own. If you are anything like me, you have been brainwashed to believe that nothing you do is ever right. You try harder and harder only to be told that you and what you are doing is not good enough or that you are not good enough. Once you read this book you will have the courage and support to take action to create a safe and healthy life.

As you read this book you will discover painful truths. You may laugh, cry, gasp, or cheer, because you can relate all too well, you will experience growth. It may be painful growth. However, you will also blossom like the beautiful being you were created to be.

I want you to know that you're loved, supported, and heard. You may feel like your voice has been silenced and stolen from you. I'm here to tell you that you have a voice.

Thank you for letting me share my story with you. I want to encourage you, empower you, inspire you, and uplift you, those who don't have a voice, and the women who have lost their lives to domestic violence and abuse.

You are not alone.

You have a soft place to land.

CHAPTER 1

Overview

"Resilience is all about being able to overcome the unexpected. Sustainability is about survival. The goal of resilience is to thrive." ~Jamais Cascio

Domestic violence is not an isolated one-time event. If you've been abused once by your spouse or partner, your risk of being further abused is extremely high. As a matter of fact, the abuse will occur more frequently and the level of abuse will escalate and become more severe. I mistakenly believed that the physical abuse I endured the first time was an isolated incident. I thought he was just under a lot of stress. I thought he made a mistake by physically abusing me. I thought that even though he choked me until I passed out. According to the Bureau of Justice Statistics, every 15 seconds in the United States a woman is beaten by her spouse or boyfriend. That is approximately 2-3million women per year. Out of these 2-3 million women, approximately 4 women are murdered and die each day as a result of the abuse.

On average, a woman leaves her spouse or boyfriend 6-7 times before she decides to leave for good. Or, unfortunately she's murdered by him before she has the chance to leave for good. My first beating occurred when I tried to explain to my husband how I didn't like the treatment I was getting from him and some of his family members. He became frustrated and wanted me to wait on him for every little thing. He claimed he could hear in my voice that I was contemplating leaving him. He said he beat me because he didn't want to lose me. He added that he would kill me if I ever thought of leaving him.

I don't want any other women to make the same mistakes that I made. My mistakes could've cost me and my daughter our lives. I didn't reach out for help when I should've. I didn't have a safe exit strategy plan. I don't want you to live in fear. I know being fearless is easier said than done, but you're not alone. I'm going to share the steps you need to take in order to survive and thrive.

I am a Survivor of 20 years of domestic abuse and violence. Domestic violence doesn't discriminate. You can be a target no matter what your race, age, religion, educational level, or your socioeconomic status is. I was ashamed to tell anyone how my husband called me names and insulted me. Here I was a professional woman with academic degrees. Ironically, I held a degree in psychology!

Domestic violence can turn you in to an emotional mess. You can become stuck not knowing what to feel and why it happened. I was in a long term relationship/marriage with someone who I loved and supported with all my heart. The good times were good but the bad times were very bad.

Our relationship started out great. He was very charming, attentive, caring, and knew all of the right things to say to get and keep me hooked on him. He was very good with his words.

However, there were red flags that I didn't recognize as warning signs, like only wanting to spend time with me and not wanting me to spend time with my friends, family or even his family, calling me degrading names and giving me the silent treatment. He criticized everything I wore and picked out my clothes because he said I needed swag.

At the time I didn't know it was abuse. I just knew it made me feel awful. I see myself as a social butterfly and he isolated me from friends and family because he wanted me all to himself. One of the tactics he used was to insult my friends so they no longer wanted to come around. These things chipped away at my self-esteem.

It wasn't until after the abuse that I began to do the work on me to fix me. That's when I realized just how low my self-esteem and self-worth had decreased.

My abuser told me stories of how he grew up watching his father beat his mother and called her bitch and other vile names. He vowed he would never ever do that to me. He had nightmares and flashbacks of his father beating his mother. He would wake up in the middle of the night drenched with sweat.

I'd comfort him and thought I could fix the pain of his past. I didn't know that boys who witness domestic violence are twice as likely to abuse their own spouse/partner and children when they become adults. I didn't know or fully understand that I was being abused until I started being physically abused.

I stayed because I thought I could "fix it" and make our relationship better. I wanted a family for our daughter so I was willing to do what I thought was necessary. I thought if I protected him from going to jail, proved my loyalty by not calling the police, and by not going to the hospital, that things would get better. But they didn't…they only got worse.

He was so good with his words. I believed him every time he said he was sorry, bought me flowers, or wrote me eloquently worded poems of apologies that were just for me. It finally got to the point that no matter what I said or did he let me know it was not good enough. He said that everything I did was "muthafuckin wrong" and there was nothing I could do to be good enough. I found myself in a repeating cycle of feeling dazed, confused, and abused.

Many people ask, "How did you let that happen?" "What did you do to make him beat you?" For a while I blamed myself. Some Place Safe, my local women's shelter, helped me begin to understand that I am not to blame. They taught me this important point. Physical and verbal abuse is not about you. It's about the abuser's internal conflicts and struggles that they battle with and carry on a daily basis.

For some time I hid the dirty little secret of shame and embarrassment that this was happening to me. I agreed with everything my abuser said for fear of what he would say or do to me if I didn't agree. I never felt "good enough" because he always found a way to make me feel bad.

Sometimes I wonder if somewhere deep down inside I knew he was capable of physically harming me in a violent rage. I once spoke to a group of women on the topic of "Know Your Worth , Change Your Life." The next week my husband beat me because the following morning after my talk, I received a call from another organization inviting me to come speak. After he beat me, he told me to run and tell my little women about that beat down. That was the moment when I realized I no longer wanted to be a fraud.

Finally, I decided to get the strength and courage to know my own worth and stand in my own truth. I wanted to begin my journey of healing. I knew I had to break the cycle if not for myself, but also for my daughter because she witnessed the abuse I endured.

So I ask all of you to join me to break the cycle of domestic violence:

- ❖ Know the red flags and protect yourself
- ❖ Call the police and don't cover up for your abuser. I covered for my abuser because I loved him and felt sorry for him … in the end, it didn't matter.
- ❖ Go to the hospital -- I didn't go to the hospital to get a medical exam. As a result, my abuser and his attorney used that against me in court stating that the abuse never happened even though our daughter witnessed the abuse and called the police. She still has nightmares and suffers from panic attacks and anxiety.
- ❖ Know that abuse is about power and control – because the abuser feels like they are losing control of you. He will hire attorneys who are like his clones to further abuse you in the court system. Together they will abuse you through social media and build a following of people (flying monkeys) who will support them in their continued abuse of you. Remember your abuser charmed and fooled you so therefore they are able to charm and fool others.
- ❖ File reports, follow-up and follow-through
- ❖ Do not return to your abuser expecting something different, it only gets worse more importantly, you are know you are worth more than the abuse you endure.

So, I share my story with you as a survivor of domestic abuse and violence because the shame does not belong to me and know that the shame does not belong to you! Forgive yourself, be kind to yourself and most importantly… know your worth and change your life!

Know the Weeds & Seeds in Your Life

I was embarrassed. I had spent my life being careful of the company that I kept. This experience forced me to take a much needed inventory of who I had allowed into my circle. I call this the Weeds & Seeds Inventory. The weeds may appear to be growing aggressively with you but they don't add value to your life and purpose. You will find that weeds will overtake you and damage you. They will smother you and suck you dry to keep you from blossoming.

At the time, you think nothing of this weed wrapping around you until you realize the grip is so tight that you've withered and you find yourself looking and feeling bad.

The seeds on the other hand are there in the time of darkness and in that darkness you will grow. Seeds are people who will pour into you and add high value to your life and purpose. Seeds are there to help you blossom and shine even in the dark times. They will grow with you, support you, help cultivate you and delight in your growth so you can develop into the best version of who you are.

After doing my weeds and seeds inventory, I was angry with myself that I didn't see some of the red flags and that I chose to ignore the red flags that I did see. All of my life, I had tried to do everything I could to not become one of the statistics that society said I would be based on where I came from.

On that first day of life-threatening physical abuse, I realized I *had* become some of the very statistics that I had tried so hard to avoid. I was devastated, 20 years of my life was gone and will never to return because someone didn't value my worth or his worth. I allowed someone to attempt to strip me of my last bit of worth that I was so desperately trying to hold on to.

I've said this many times, women who haven't experienced physical abuse, verbal abuse, or emotional abuse, don't fully understand what a woman who has experienced abuse is going through. To them, it is cut and dry, black and white.

My long time friend told me she doesn't understand why I allowed him to do what he did to me and why I ignored the red flags. I didn't know the red flags were red flags until he physically beat me down. She kept telling me that I needed to leave my home and move. She went on to tell me that I act like I'm stuck and don't have a plan. Financially, I couldn't just jump and move. I had no clue where I'd move to. I'd already learned very quickly how dangerous it is to abruptly leave in the middle of the night with no plan. I didn't have a place to stay and the shelters were full and I didn't know anyone.

What I did know was that I didn't want him to kill me.

A woman that I thought was my friend proved to be otherwise. We met during my college school days. She had confided in me how she fled from her husband because he was physically abusive. I can remember thinking to myself very briefly, would my husband ever do that and I quickly dismissed the thought and continued listening to her story.

A few years later when my husband began to abuse me, I confided in her because I assumed she would understand my situation. Instead, she told me I was living a lie and that I was a fraud. She said if she ever caught wind of me speaking to other women about knowing their worth, she would expose me. She claimed she would tell everyone I was a fraud and that my husband was at home beating me. In her final blow, she told me she was disgusted with me posting positive messages on social media when my life was a train wreck. She also informed me she had "unfriended" me and stopped following me on social media because she couldn't stomach watching me live a lie. After that phone conversation, I didn't hear from her again until she called me a year and a half later.

I asked myself "How could my so called "friends" be so cold and cruel?" Over the years, they had dumped their problems in my ear and lap and I supported them unconditionally and non-judgmentally. I didn't have any friends and I was trying to hold onto these two for dear life.

I finally had to be real with me and re-evaluate my friendship with these two women. I asked myself, " When these women ask me how I'm doing and I'm honest, does it help me to be honest about my feelings when they're so critical of my raw feelings and honesty? Or is it a setback for me emotionally?

It was a setback for me emotionally because I could no longer live a lie and pretend I was okay when I really wasn't. These friends didn't understand what I was going through emotionally, physically, financially, spiritually, and overall as a human being. I had to let them go until I could begin to heal on my own.

No one can tell you how to heal or how long it should take you to heal. You know what you have gone through and no one else has experienced your journey. When so-called friends and family throw you away or leave you because you're not healing the way they think you should heal, let them go. They're not your true friends. As for family, let them go as well. The right people will come into your life and become your family. Family is not always about being related by blood.

Yes, I was like so many women of domestic violence and abuse. I came back home after I left. The last time I came home I knew from what the policeman and the therapist told me that if I didn't file for a protection order I was going to be a dead woman.

The last time I came back, I didn't come back saying, "Ooooh baby let's make this work." I just wanted to merely exist and stay alive. I was so exhausted and tired of playing his mind games and kissing up to him and his family hoping they would be nice to me. The lesson I learned with these 2 "friends" is that if someone can't support you when you're down, then you don't need them around. At least not while you are at your lowest point in life.

For me, I don't want to be around someone who turns their back on me or has no compassion when I am at my lowest point in life. I had called several family members to tell them about my situation. I wanted to be accounted for since I had almost been killed and had my life threatened. No one in my family called back to check on me. There were also "church people" who heard through the grapevine what was going in my life and they would call me as if they were concerned. Once they got my business, they didn't call back. Not even with a prayer. This experience truly strengthened my faith, belief, and trust in my Higher Power. It made me know that when everyone else turns their back on me, God is there for me to depend on. That is truly what has gotten me through this.

Well We *Were* Movin' On Up

I spent so much time replaying different events in my head and trying to understand how this thing called a relationship that we exchanged vows for could go so far left in the wrong direction so quickly. I kept getting caught up in the shouldas, couldas, and wouldas, of how I could have prevented it and blah, blah, blah…

Then one day I decided to stop punishing myself so harshly for what someone else chose to do to me. I was on a mission to figure out why and how I could let such a horrific thing happen to me. I wanted to know what it was about me that attracted such a person? What was it within me that accepted bad degrading behavior for 20 years? What was it about me that even though I knew I was worth more than what I experienced in this so-called relationship, yet I still stayed. I stayed and accepted lying, cheating, manipulation, rape, deceit, and ultimately physical beatings.

I was so dazed and confused and couldn't understand how I grew up in the hood and went to one of the roughest and toughest high schools in the city of Pittsburgh and here I was in this situation. I survived the early 90's when gang violence, shootings, and drugs, were rampant and at its highest peak and here I was in this situation.

I just couldn't wrap my brain around how I had "nevah" been thrown a beating like the one I had initially received and getting a Lifetime "beat down" in my Lifetime looking home and my Lifetime looking neighborhood that I had worked so hard for. I asked myself how is it that I could get off of the 81B Lincoln (Public Transportation in Pittsburgh) at night and stand and wait for a ½ hour for the 74A Squirrel Hill/Homewood bus to take me down the street and not once did I get beaten up or called a "bitch" by the crack heads and thugs that walked by me and mumbled "Sup". I had gone to school, got a job, and worked my way up the ranks to a good annual salary and I thought we were like George and Weezy, we were movin' on up.

The Painful Journey of Self-Discovery

Unfortunately, it all came crashing down faster than the elevator in that deluxe apartment in the sky. As a result of my pain and brokenness from this experience, I needed to heal. I could have turned to drugs, alcohol, or some other form of self-destructive abuse that would continue to perpetuate the cycle of domestic violence that I had been so brutally and instantaneously thrust into. I didn't make that choice. Instead, I had a spiritual awakening that forced me on a much welcomed spiritual journey of self-discovery.

Some people may say this is over the top. On my spiritual journey, I have learned to not care what other people say or think, especially about me. Since then I read 100+ books and listened to over 30 audio books within a 1 year timeframe to inspire and guide me.

I made up my mind that enough is enough. I was ready to do the work to go on a life-long journey of self-love, self-care, self-compassion, self-awareness. No, it is not self-ish. My vision and my goal is to share my story of how I came to know my worth with other women who are in situations where they need to SPEAK Up and Get Out!

I don't know if it's an issue of needing more resources or not. What I do know is that there needs to be more action oriented awareness to prevent women from being or becoming a victim of domestic violence. I asked myself, "Why is it that when a woman is being physically abused one of the first things she's asked is "Why don't you just leave?" My question is, "Why can't he leave or stop?" or "Why can't he change?"

I want to help you grow, heal, and embark on a journey of true self-discovery to learn how to know your own worth. For some of you, this process will be just as painful as the experience that has brought you to the point of needing to know your true worth. It's all about healing the wounds of your life and undergoing a transformation. No more playing small, no more hiding, no more living a watered down version of yourself. Be authentically you!

It's time to be the best version of you. You are enough, so know your worth. In chapters 4 through 8, I'll explain my SPEAK Formula that will equip and empower you with the knowledge you need to **S**ave yourself, **P**repare a safety plan, **E**nforce boundaries you create, **A**sk questions from professionals, and **K**eep your information and documents safe.

CHAPTER 2

What is Abuse? The Turmoil Beneath the Water

"Abuse doesn't come from people's inability to resolve conflicts but from one person's decision to claim a higher status than another." ~Lundy Bancroft

---

Abuse is Not Just Physical

In this chapter I want to discuss the different types of abuse. As I mentioned previously, I didn't know I was being abused until I was physically abused. However, there were red flags that I didn't know were warning signs, like only wanting to spend time with me and not wanting me to spend time with my friends, family or even his family. Calling me degrading names, giving me the silent treatment, criticizing everything I wore, and picking out my clothes because he said I needed swag.

At the time, I didn't know it was abuse I just knew it made me feel awful. It was painful because I was isolated from friends and family. I consider myself to be a social butterfly and this just didn't feel good. One of the tactics he would use was to insult my friends and family so they would no longer want to come around. This would also cause conflict between me and my friends because they felt like I should speak up and defend them against him.

Whenever we were around my family he would insult them with jokes or act as though he was so offended by someone that we would have to leave. He would also say he didn't feel well so we would have to leave functions early. He would also make our daughter ask me who I was talking to on the phone.

He would always monitor my telephone calls and internet activity. He worked different shifts every week for his job. Whenever he worked the evening or night shift, I would have to go to bed with him because he said he needed me next to him in order to fall asleep. Sometimes I would sneak out of the bed so I could help our daughter with homework, getting her dinner, or preparing her for school the next day. When he would wake up and discover I was not beside him, he would get very angry. He would apologize for what he called "busting a brat move", but he stressed that he didn't like when I am not close by.

No matter what shift he worked, he would leave the house and call back home within 15-20 minutes to ask me what I was doing. During his work shift he would call numerous times to ask me what I was doing, why I didn't answer the phone, or to find out if I was talking to someone on the phone. One day, while working on my doctoral degree, I experienced a block in writing. I decided to take our daughter to the local safari petting zoo.

My abuser called my cell phone, and he was angry because he called the house and I didn't answer. I told him where we were, and he told me to get my ass home. He was angry because I didn't ask him for permission first or let him know ahead of time that we were going to go. He told me we would go the following week with him. The following week, we went back to the animal safari park, and he was not in a good mood because it was hot, he was sweating, and the animals smelled bad. Many times my daughter and I didn't go anywhere without him because he was afraid we would get hurt, and he didn't want anyone to bother us.

I was not allowed to do much of anything alone. My abuser would also come and sit on the edge of our tub and talk to me if I took too long in the bathroom. He would also stress how much he liked to be with me and around me all of the time. In the beginning I was flattered and thought he was just showing me how much he loved me. Most of the time movie nights consisted of him always deciding what movies or television shows we could watch. If he didn't like it, we didn't watch it. If I suggested a movie or television show, he would tell me it was "garbage", and we were going to watch something else.

I once called his cousin to find out if she could drive me and my daughter to an outlet mall to go school shopping. She was very excited about our mini trip. My abuser was upset because I didn't get permission from him first. He was angry because he said that I knew he would say no to me spending time with her. Yes, he was correct. He was upset with her because she was interacting with someone that he had an issue with.

He said she was not loyal to him because she continued talking to a young girl that he felt betrayed him. He then accused me of not being loyal to him because I was talking to his cousin and I even went as far as to spend the day with her. While we were on the road and at the shopping mall, he called me several times wanting to know what we were talking about and when I was coming home. The interesting part was that he was at work. Our daughter and I would have been at home alone not doing anything.

His cousin commented about how much he called. She also commented about me calling him to get permission to make a purchase for myself. I guess at the time neither one of us knew I was in the cycle of domestic violence and being completely controlled by him. She said she was happy to be single she couldn't be bothered with having to report in to a man like that.

His cousin and I used to talk every morning. We would have great conversations. She and I would laugh, talk, text, send emails, and we really bonded. I didn't mention our conversations to him because one, I didn't want to be forced to repeat every detail of our conversations and two, I didn't want him to make me stop talking to her. Our conversations ended when he started working the afternoon shift.

He was home in the mornings and he began questioning me about who I was talking to. He accused me of talking to other men and accused me of being with other women. I begged him to believe me that I was really talking to his cousin. I had never cheated or given him a reason to make such an accusation. Shortly after, his cousin stopped calling me, and I didn't want to betray him so I didn't call her anymore. The next time I saw her, she was rolling her eyes at me. I never knew what happened. I now suspect he must have said something to her about me to turn her against me.

It began to occur to me that I no longer had a voice. My slogan to him became, "Whatever you want to do is fine with me. Let's rock and roll. I've got your back no matter what." I realized this was the best way to keep him happy and in a good mood. These things chipped away at my self-esteem. I had no life, no friends, and no family to interact with. It wasn't until I began to do the work on me to fix me after the abuse that I realized how low my self-esteem and self-worth had diminished.

Throughout this book you will learn about the following characteristics, red flags, and behaviors to help you identify a controlling abusive man.

- Cocky/Arrogant
- Lies
- Envious/Jealous of you or others
- Always thinks someone is jealous of him
- Selfish
- Self-centered
- Cheats on you with someone else
- Cheats when playing video games or games
- Hates to lose a game especially to children
- Has temper tantrums like a toddler
- Does not respect your boundaries
- Manipulative
- Mean
- Disrespectful
- Rude
- Inconsiderate; Does not consider you or your feelings

- Has no goals
- Gossips
- Sneaky
- Knows everything
- Spineless with others but dominant with you or children
- Bully
- Insecure
- Publicly shares information from your private conversations
- Highly Competitive; has to win no matter what
- Pins you down or restrains you to keep you from leaving the house or room
- Intentionally does things you have asked him not to do

Emotional/Verbal Abuse

Emotional abuse is just as unhealthy and toxic as physical abuse. No, emotional abuse and verbal abuse don't leave cuts and bruises, but they are very harmful to the mind and soul. Emotional and verbal abuse molests your mind and rapes your soul leaving your spirit broken. Emotional and verbal abuse can cause physical health problems and emotional pain that can take years to heal.

Verbal and emotional abuse can be so damaging that you begin to believe the negative things your spouse/partner says about you. You begin to think you are not good enough, that people don't really like you, or you are an ugly bearded bitch. Calling me a "bearded bitch" was one of his favorite things to say to me. He thought it was hilarious. To me, it was hurtful and cruel because he knew I suffered for years battling female facial hair.

Your inner spirit may be speaking to you telling you it doesn't feel right, but because of love and other possible reasons you continue to stay in a toxic relationship. It is very frustrating for an abuser to brag about you to the public, yet degrade and demean you behind closed doors. This was something my mother would do and it irked me.

I wanted people to see the behind closed doors man that I had to suffer through. Over time, this type of treatment begins to make you feel as though you are not good enough and causes you to lose your confidence, self-esteem, self-worth, and even your self- respect. As a result, you begin to self-blame, self-abuse, and believe you are responsible for your spouse's/partner's behavior.

Emotional and verbal abuse consists of non-physical behaviors that slowly chips away at your self-esteem and self-worth.

These include but are not limited to the following:

- Insults
- Belittling you
- Intimidation
- Not respecting your boundaries
- Threats
- Ignoring your wishes
- Degrading you
- Constantly monitoring you
- Always checking in on you
- Excessive calls and texts
- Stalking
- Screaming
- Name calling
- Isolating you from friends, family, and neighbors and even from your own children
- Making accusations about you

- Blaming you
- Degrading you
- Lying to you or lying on you
- Betraying your confidence
- Not taking responsibility for his abusive behavior
- Attacks your character
- Destroy your credibility
- Publicly humiliating you through inappropriate jokes
- Finding humor in your fear
- Threatening your loved ones
- Insulting your loved ones
- Putting you down
- Withholding information
- Making sarcastic comments or remarks
- Slandering you on Social Media
- Using excessive profanity
- Not keeping promises
- Being secretive
- Intentionally forgetting
- Being jealous
- Destroying your personal property
- Cheating
- Ignoring you when you speak
- Sulking and feeling sorry for himself to make you feel guilty
- Walking away from you while you are talking as a form of control
- Beating your dog or some other family pet
- Back handed compliments

- Passive-Aggressive
- Pretends to have forgotten something very important
- Remembers things that only benefit him

Our lives turned upside down when he decided to have a surgery at the local hospital as opposed to going to one of the larger cities. The complications from the surgery caused him to experience major health complications and a horrible change in being able to enjoy life. As a result of this surgery, he ended up with a very deep infected wound, PICC line, and a colostomy bag. Prior to him getting the colostomy bag, he enjoyed passing gas in my face. He would walk by me as I sat on the couch, and he would pass gas. He would pass gas in the bed and trap me under the cover, in the middle of eating he enjoyed passing gas with no consideration of me and our daughter. He would sometimes laugh until tears rolled down his face as I gagged or vomited from the smell.

The more I would ask him not to do these things the more he would do it or he would get angry with me and tell me I never wanted to have any fun. I love having fun but this is just not my idea of having a fun time. Once he got the colostomy bag his behavior got even worse. He would burp/let the air out of his colostomy bag into my face while I would be sleeping in the bed or just laying there trying to relax.

In the middle of eating dinner he would lift up his shirt to show me and our daughter his poop through the clear colostomy bag. He would then laugh and say, "Look Babycakes/LadyBug/Doll (or whatever name he decided to call me at the time), I am playing with my poop. Wanna feel it? I can feel chicken; look you can see my chicken and peas!" He would then laugh and burp the bag as we tried to eat. Burping the bag consists of letting the air out of the colostomy bag which is the equivalent of passing gas. By this time, I wouldn't even bother asking him not to do this because he would accuse me of not loving him because he had a colostomy bag. No, he didn't physically harm me with these actions but it did cause me emotional discomfort and frustration.

The following examples are tactics that are used when someone is emotionally or verbally abusing you. I have included my real life examples because I don't want you to think you are the only person who has experienced this type of abuse. I share these examples from a place of strength. No matter how lonely you may feel, you are not alone on your journey. You are loved and you matter. These are definitely warning signs and red flags to identify whether you are or have been emotionally or verbally abused. Answer the following questions:

1. Does your Spouse/Partner call you derogatory names or put you down?

2. Does he call you any of these names or similar?

3. Does he use your insecurities about your physical appearance against you?

Here are some examples:

- Bitch
- Crazy
- Silly bitch
- Stupid
- Dr. Bitch
- Fat pig
- Fat
- A fucking…
- A bad wife
- Mentally ill
- Dumb bitch
- Dirty bitch
- Nut job
- Bearded bitch

- Know it all
- A piece of shit
- A cold hearted bitch
- A lesbian/gay
- Sensitive
- Juggernaut
- Nut job
- Would treat you better if you were a whore
- Mock you
- Nutsy
- Give you the silent treatment
- Slut
- Big Bear
- Loser
- Schmuck
- Yell and scream at you? Remember a person does not always have to yell and scream to insult or degrade you. They can be experts at what I have experienced to be considered "nice nasty". These people set out to hurt you emotionally with a smile on their face and a very calm cool attitude. They say very mean and hurtful things that cut you to the white meat with a smile on their face.
- Embarrass you on purpose in public or in front of other people
- Make you feel guilty for spending time with your friends and family? Sometimes they won't flat out tell you not to but their actions through sulking, the silent treatment, or other non-verbal ways let you know they don't agree with you.
- Constantly tell you what to wear or criticize what you wear.
- Use social media to control, intimidate, or humiliate you.

- Blame you for their abusive behavior or unhealthy habits.
- Stalk you at work, home, or want to know where you are at all times.
- Threatens to commit suicide if you don't do what they want you to do or if you want to end the relationship.
- Threatens to kill or harm your pet or people you love and care about.
- Force you to have sex, make you feel guilty for not wanting to have sex, and acts immature by not taking "NO" for an answer.
- Threatens to tell people your secrets.
- Lies on you and spreads rumors to turn people against you.
- Threatens to kill you, divorce you, take everything you have, or try to get you fired from your job.
- Calmly threatens you with a smile or insult you in a joking manner.
- Claims to be sick or really is sick and tells you that you're the only one who can help him get well.

When you are constantly being told everything you do is wrong, you will begin to question your goals, dreams, and accomplishments. Somehow you will contemplate giving up on things that you once found pleasure in doing. I was definitely in the cycle of domestic violence and didn't have a clue. I had broken up with him many times before and when I fled in the middle of the night, like many times before I came back home to him. The cycle of domestic violence has three parts. As I stated previously, verbal and emotional abuse are the appetizers an abuser serves you before devouring you with their main course of physical abuse or death.

The first stage is tension building – During this phase tension begins to build with an abuser who is having issues related to money, health, loss of job which is tied to money or relationship issues with his family members. This is when verbal and emotional abuse begins. The abuser's spouse or partner falls in to the trap of trying to "fix" the situation by pleasing her abuser, or agreeing with her abuser to avoid an abusive or uncomfortable confrontation.

The second stage is Physical Abuse/Battering - In this stage, it can take 2 weeks, 1 year, 5 years, or in my case 20 years before a woman is physically abused. I have worked with women who had been married for over 30 years when they were blindsided by physical abuse. Battering begins when an abuser feels like he is losing power and control over you. The goal of physical abuse is to beat you back into submission.

The third stage is the Honeymoon Phase - During this phase your abuser may show a glimpse of remorse to convince you not to leave. He may also not take responsibility for his actions and blame you for his behavior. He may even promise that he will never physically or verbally abuse you again. He may do things for you that you always wanted him to do but never did. This is to convince you that he has changed. He will be nice, affectionate, and patient long enough to rebuild trust with you. He wants to reassure you that the two of you have a strong bond that can't be broken. Therefore, it is not necessary for you to leave the relationship.

When my daughter and I returned home from fleeing in the middle of the night, he started off being very nice cooking, buying our favorite foods, and being overly nice on his very best behavior. He did have several times where the post-surgery mean cruel guy popped out. Overall, he was nicer to me than he had been in years.

I was very surprised because leading up to me coming back home, our phone conversations consisted of him being very verbally abusive. The more I begged him to stop calling me names and being so cold the more he would call me names and tell me how horrible of a person I was for leaving. I shouldn't have made contact with him after I left. However, I did and because of this I returned home.

In the days after returning home, he and I were sitting in the family room and he dropped the remote control. It fell on the floor right beside his foot. Instead of him picking it up, he called our daughter from upstairs in her room to come downstairs to pick up the remote control for him.

After she picked up the remote control she sat down on the couch across from us as she continued reading a book on her phone. He then looks at me and said, "I hope she is not like Ray Donovan's daughter." I asked, "Who is Ray Donovan?" He explained he was a character from a television show whose daughter is a, "Whore taking photos of her ass and sending them to boys." I asked him why he would say something like that about her and especially in front of her? He began to laugh and tell jokes about our daughter being a whore. Tears began to stream down her face as she said she was going to the bathroom. He began to taunt her and ask why she was crying. After he left for the evening, she finally came out of the bathroom and said she only stayed in there because she was tired of him always hurting us.

Two weeks later he and I went to a counseling session with a therapist. This was supposed to be my own personal session because he told me I was crazy and needed help. To ensure that I didn't try to run or escape again he called it a marriage couple's session. He also wanted to make sure that I didn't tell her the truth. His goal was to intimidate the entire time to keep me from telling the therapist about the abuse. The therapist did explain in the session that she didn't counsel couples but she would ask me questions directly.

He didn't like that I told the therapist how his mother would ask for money and steal/take things from our home including my personal things. He didn't like that I also told the therapist that he beat me, has told countless lies, and cheated for years. I was tired and I wanted to fix my marriage because it was broken. He got angry because I told the truth. He went to grab me, called me names, and stormed out of her office.

The therapist was just as afraid as I was. After he left, she said it is clear that he has a very bad temper. If he is comfortable enough to attempt to physically harm you in front of me, you are a dead woman if you are alone with him. Our daughter was in the waiting room. When I came out to check on her she was in tears. She said, "Dad just walked by me and gave me the 2 finger peace sign salute and said 'I'm out.'"

Protecting your child or children from abuse is just as important as protecting yourself. I will be honest with you, had it not been for my daughter, I wouldn't have done anything to protect myself. My daughter would plead with me to see that how I was being treated was wrong.

Sexual Abuse

The US Department of Justice reports 76% of women who reported being raped over the age of 18 had been violated by their current or former husband or boyfriend. Rape is a form of sexual abuse. Sexual abuse can be described as being forced, persuaded, intimidated, or pressured into having sexual contact with someone against your wishes. I always thought rape was committed by a stranger.

During my pregnancy with our daughter I suffered with hyperemesis gravidarum. I experienced excessive nausea, vomiting, and weight loss during the entire 9 months of my pregnancy. At one point I was experiencing cramping and bleeding. The doctor instructed me not to engage in any sexual activity or anything that would involve penetration. My abuser was with me during the appointment and heard everything the doctor said.

This didn't matter to my abuser. As we left the doctor's office, my abuser asked me what I expected him to do. I didn't know what he meant initially. He told me I was going to give it up. Later that evening, he told me we were going to have sex. I repeated to him what the doctor said but he didn't care. My abuser forced me to have sex, he didn't care that I was crying, and he didn't care about the well-being of our unborn child. Just as the doctor predicted, I began to bleed and cramp. I asked my abuser to take me to the hospital and his response was, "Suck it up kid."

Like many women who are in abusive relationships, they leave 6 to 7 times before they are gone for good or murdered. Once the baby was born, I left him because of how he treated me not only during this particular incident but throughout the entire pregnancy he was cruel and insensitive. He was very angry that I broke up with him. He went on what I have come to learn what is called a psychopathic narcissistic smear campaign.

We will discuss smear campaigns in a later chapter. He lied on me and talked negatively about me to his family, friends, and anyone else that would listen. He also told his best friend and his wife that I had disappeared with the baby, and he didn't know where we were. This was not true because he showed up at my job. When I got off from work as I was walking down the street he jumped up from behind a car he was hiding behind. I hurried up and got away. I went and hid at my sister's house with the baby.

He called my mother and she told him where I was. So he knew where we were. I then scheduled visits for him to see our daughter at my mother's home without me being present. For a while he wouldn't show up because he said he wanted us to visit as a family. He kept trying to pressure me into taking him back and I finally folded.

My abuser's female cousin called me one day and asked me why I broke up with him. I explained to her it was personal and that I had very good reasons. This was his attempt to use someone else to reel me back into a relationship with him. After she kept probing me, I finally told her what happened during my pregnancy. I also explained his addiction to lying about everything big and small, constantly cheating, and stealing from my brother-in-law. This caused tension between me and my sister because I defended my husband. After I told her how he forced me to have sex prior to and during my pregnancy, she explained to me that she once worked for a women's crisis hotline and it does not matter if it is a spouse, partner, or stranger -rape is rape.

She continued to tell me that no means no. She was in shock that he had done this to me. I was in shock that it happened to me. A few years later she asked me again, and I told her the same thing. She said her heart was broken to know that he would do something like that. Even though some of his family members knew of his behavior towards me, they continued to turn a blind eye and support him. No one tried to tell him his behavior was wrong. They wouldn't speak up to him even when they were personally insulted by him through his mean jokes.

I can't stress enough that when you are in an abusive relationship you have to know who you can trust and confide in. Many family members and friends have a hard time accepting and believing that their loved one can be so cruel and mean. If you are in an abusive relationship, it is very important to contact the National Domestic Violence Hotline at 1-800-799-SAFE (7233) or visit www.NCADV.org. They can also provide you the information for your local women's shelter. You are not alone.

The following are a few examples of sexual abuse:

- Threatening or intimidating you to have sexual contact
- Refusing to use a condom or not allowing you to use another form of contraception
- Having rough sex or playing rough during sexual contact
- Making you perform a sexual act
- Trying to persuade you to have sex with other people

Financial Abuse

Financial abuse is a form of domestic abuse that can place you in a position of lacking the necessary resources to be independent in a relationship. Financial abuse can sometimes create a barrier that makes it difficult for a woman to have the confidence she needs to leave an abusive relationship. Financial abuse is not always blatant or obvious. It can be done in a very smooth, charming, persuasive, and subtle manner. There are different ways you can be financially abused by a spouse. Financial abuse can happen in any of the following ways but not just limited to this list. These are just some examples to give you an idea of how you could possibly be financially abused.

Does your spouse or partner:

- Not want you to have a job?
- Discourage you from having an income?
- Control what you can spend your money on?
- Refuse to allow you to have your own bank account?

- Won't permit your name to be on a joint bank account?
- Won't allow you to access any bank accounts?
- Allow you a set amount of money each week or month?
- Force you to open credit cards in your name only and charge high balances?
- Intentionally not pay bills in your name to ruin your credit so that you have bad credit?
- Create large amounts of debts on joint accounts without your knowledge?
- Make you work for the family business for minimal to no pay, no retirement savings fund, or benefits?
- Force you to work 1-2 jobs while he is unemployed yet you don't see any of the money you have worked for?
- Control your paychecks by making you give all of the money without ever seeing a penny of it?
- Force you to show receipts for all of your purchases?
- Make you account for all of the money you spend?
- Won't permit you to have money to purchase food, clothing, toiletries, medication, or basic necessities?
- Freely purchases what he wants or needs or makes sure others are provided for but does not allow you to do the same?
- Offers to assist you with something or does something for you in the name of "help," but you know there are strings attached, or he expects the same in return?
- Secretive about the details of the money, and what the money is being used for?
- Encourage you to NOT take promotions on your job?
- Steal money from you or your family members?
- Joking about keeping you in the kitchen bare foot and pregnant?
- Does not care about keeping your credit in good standing?

- Not give you money for food, clothing, medication, or other essential items?
- Spend money that you are saving for the child or children?
- Treat you to expensive items and expect some kind of favor in return?
- Make you turn down promotions so your income won't increase or surpass his income?
- Prevent you from investing your money to increase your wealth and financial independence?
- Make you pay for life insurance policies when he has no intentions of keeping you as a beneficiary?

If you answered yes to any of these questions, you could be the victim of financial abuse. I highly suggest that you get on the phone and contact your local women's domestic violence shelter or the National Domestic Violence Hotline at 1-800-799-SAFE if any of these things are happening to you. There are Domestic Violence Advocates you can talk to any time of the day or night. They are there 24/7. I would call frequently, sometimes just to talk because I was ashamed to tell my friends and family. The ones I did reach out to didn't understand and were very judgmental. When you call the hotlines there is no need to feel ashamed or judged. They understand and want to help you.

I will share with you my experience of financial abuse. Financial abuse by a spouse/partner is not always about whoever makes the most money or controls the money. It makes me cringe every time I hear people say, "Oh she is staying for the money or the lifestyle." If you are reading this book you most likely know it's not about the money or the lifestyle. It is about the emotional ties we have to our abuser and the amount of brainwashing we have endured. My abuser would always charge items to my credit card and tell me that he knew as long as I had credit card debt I would never leave.

He would also make it very clear that if I ever tried to leave him he would take more than half of everything I had. He also threatened to lie on me to get full custody of our daughter, so I would have to pay him child support and spousal support. These things were never said in an angry tone, they were always said in a joking manner, yet he made sure I knew he would follow through with his plan if I ever tried to leave him. Many of these threats would be made in the middle of having sex or during a happy time.

My abuser's parents would always ask us for money. In the beginning I thought it was just because of an emergency. After quite a bit of time passed I realized it was a frequent and persistent pattern. They considered us their personal bank to use for frivolous spending. I didn't understand why they were always asking for money. What I did know is that I got tired of always having to pay their bills, pay their rent for their apartment, rent for their furniture, rent for their appliances, paying for his dad's cigarettes, and their overall careless overspending. They rented their television, washer, dryer, microwave, furniture, computer, and always had a so-called financial crisis for us to bail them out of.

They even wanted us to add them to our cell phone service account. He also had a cousin who would call and ask us for money on a regular basis. She even asked for us to pay for her rent. I may have considered it had she not been forced to resign from her job for selling client information out of the establishment's confidential database. I no longer wanted to financially bail out people who were careless about their personal financial well-being.

I had finally had enough. I told my abuser we were no longer going to give them money or pay anyone else's bills. We also gave money to my abuser's mother so she could pay the bills of her youngest sister who never held a steady form of employment. I tried to explain to him that we couldn't continue to allow them to drain us dry financially. After giving them money we didn't have a sufficient amount of money to save for ourselves. We didn't have anyone to turn to if we found ourselves in a financial bind. We had to be able to save money so we could be our own rescue. Enough was enough. When my abuser was sick and in the hospital for a long period of time his father would throw hints about needing and wanting money. This was a common occurrence, and this time I refused to give in and hand out any money. I knew where the conversation was headed, and I told him that with my abuser being sick we could no longer pay their bills. I knew he didn't like my response. A few days later my abuser had finally awakened from a semi-conscious state. He had only been awake for approximately 3 hours after being unconscious and semi-conscious in the weeks leading up to this point.

Within those 3 hours his dad began to signify at me. He nitpicked everything I said to the point where I finally asked him if he had an issue with me that he wanted to discuss. He immediately got angry, stood up, told me he would put lead in my head, and balled his fists up in my face telling me that he would put something on me as my daughter was lying on my lap and chest. My abuser attempted to get out of bed to protect me. He told his father that he wouldn't abuse his wife like he did his mother.

My abuser's mother was on the phone in the hallway. When she heard the commotion, she came running into the room and made her husband leave. I told all of them that his father was no longer allowed to come to our home and this incident was the last straw. I also believed his father grew angry because I had already told my abuser and his father that I was tired of them using me and talking to me as if I didn't matter. They were only nice to me when they wanted money. I was willing to help my abuser get back on his feet after the surgery but there needed to be some serious changes in the way they treated me.

If they couldn't respect me all of the time and not just be nice to me when they wanted something; then we needed to make some major changes. I no longer wanted them in my home if they couldn't respect me, and I definitely wouldn't be visiting with them anymore. I didn't want my abuser to feel like he had to choose between me and his family. I was willing to remove myself from this toxic situation.

When we first purchased our home, my abuser's parents came over every day in the name of "help." Their mentality was, if they help you then they are entitled to control you, take items from our home without asking, and feel entitled to know about every aspect of what was happening in our personal lives. My abuser's mother even went as far as asking our daughter at 7 years old if she could hear her mom and dad having sex. When my daughter told me I was shocked. However, I was not floored because his aunt who is also an in-law had forewarned me that that side of the family will get your child alone and ask them questions to find out what is going on in your personal life. These people had no boundaries.

They have no respect for others. The respect they do give is only enough to get something they want from someone. They acted as if they owned us. It was more of, "I like you only because of what you can give me or do for me". My abuser and I had a running joke every time they called because they only called when they wanted money. We would look at the caller ID and say, "Wonder how much money they want this time?" Even though we joked about it, my abuser expressed how embarrassing it was to him that they didn't handle their finances properly. He felt torn between taking care of home and taking care of them. He said the pressure of it all was completely weighing him down. It weighed him down sometimes to the point of him having frequent mood swings.

Eventually, my abuser and I began falling behind on our own financial responsibilities. Some of his family members would make him feel guilty because we stopped giving money to them. He said it was too much pressure and felt manipulated and forced to continue giving money every time they asked even when our own bills needed to be paid. He always felt obligated to bail his parents out of an unnecessary financial bind. They knew he felt indebted to them, and they continued to manipulate him and make him feel guilty if he said no.

When I would say no to them, he would get angry and treat me very badly by verbally abusing me, calling me names, and using personal things that I shared with him against me. He would also emotionally abuse me by giving me the silent treatment, refusing to have sex, or giving me backhanded compliments.

"Oh, you look nice, but you are not leaving this house with those red shoes on. As a matter of fact, you need to just throw them away. Those joints are ugly!" He would laugh through the entire sentence until he saw the hurt and humiliation in my eyes. I didn't want to lose his love, and wanted to prove to him that I was loyal. So I complied with their financial requests even though I didn't want to.

I have always been a saver when it comes to my money. It is very important to be conscious of your money. The mistake I made was allowing him to dictate how the money was spent. I even stopped contributing to my retirement plan. While he was sick he suggested that I stopped contributing to my retirement plan, so the amount of my net pay would increase. Even though I resisted the suggestion, he convinced me that we could rely on his retirement fund. This made absolutely no sense to me, yet I still went along with it.

I can't stress enough the importance of being mindful of your money and in control of your own money. I also suggest having what I call a secret stash or a bank account that your spouse or partner knows nothing about. I was stuck in a cycle of wanting to be transparent with my husband to prove my loyalty. As a result, I didn't have a secret stash of money set aside that he didn't know about. This was a huge mistake because when I was blindsided by the physical abuse, I had no extra money set aside to thrive financially.

I am going to share with you a list of tactics that are used when you are being financially abused. Some of these I have experience firsthand. Before I share this list, you should also know that a spouse/partner can create a situation as I described to keep you from saving money and becoming financially independent. As women, some of us have fears around money or finances because we are not familiar with how to budget, save, or invest. I highly suggest you build or rebuild a healthy relationship with your money. Learn how to save money, invest your money, and definitely hide your money because in some states no matter who makes the money, the money is viewed as jointly owned. In the case of a divorce you will be required to divide the money equally.

Financial Abuse In The Court System By Abuser

I woke up one morning feeling awful (emotionally, spiritually, and physically). Mornings for me were awful. I was thankful to wake up and see another day, but I didn't enjoy waking up to the emotional pain of it all. I couldn't believe my life had taken such a drastic turn. I really think having to go to a court ordered parenting class set me back in more ways than one. The class was good however, it focused on communication, cooperation, and agreeing on visitation. After the class, I approached the instructor about my specific case.

The instructor told me since I had a Protection Order that protected both me and my daughter; there was no need for me to have attended the class. He further explained that it made absolutely no sense for me to have attended the class. He also stated that he couldn't understand why the court would order me to go to the class considering I was granted a 5 year protection order.

The instructor informed me that my husband must have requested that I take the class. Otherwise the court wouldn't have ordered me to take it. At that moment I realized, here I am with almost not a dime left to my name, and my soon to be ex-husband requested for me to take a class that I didn't have the money to pay for. I was struggling to get by. He knew I was scraping by financially. This was just another way for him to continue to financially abuse me.

As I have said so many times before, I didn't know I was being abused until I started getting beat. I knew what I was experiencing didn't make me feel good. It left me feeling frustrated, hurt, sad, and angry. I didn't know to classify the mistreatment I was experiencing as abuse. The physical abuse I was enduring was the second to the last stop on the route of domestic violence.

Far too many women stay in an abusive relationship, and their life is ended on the last stop of domestic violence when they are murdered by their husband or partner. A woman from the Domestic Violence Advocacy group in Washington, D.C. told me I was lucky to be alive. She told me most women who are strangled and pass out oftentimes die several hours later after being strangled. She also explained the difference between being choked and strangled.

During the divorce, I got a call from my attorney saying that my husband wanted me to get permission from him first before I could file my taxes. During our marriage he would always charge items on my credit card in my name only. He would then laugh and say, "As long as you have debt on your credit card I know you're not going anywhere woman." He would also laugh and say, "You are the only one that cares about your credit. I have filed for bankruptcy before so fees and penalties are not a big deal to me." He and his attorney never did provide the documents I needed for us to file our taxes jointly. This was the first time I had ever been late filing my taxes.

Financial & Spiritual Abuse

After fleeing in the middle of the night, I lost my job. I didn't think about any consequences of leaving without a plan. I just wanted to live. I didn't want him to finish me off and kill me like he said he would. I was exhausted from living in fear under the same roof with him. I didn't know what would set him off and walking on eggshells became too much for me to handle. Once I lost my job the pastor from my husband's family church stopped communicating with me. When I came back home I didn't tell my husband I got my job back. My employer was gracious enough to tell me if I came back to the state I could have my job back. I didn't have any other place to go so I chose to go back home to what was familiar.

I withheld this information from my abuser. I didn't tell him I was employed again. I began to learn about narcissistic abuse, and how one of the traits of people with a narcissistic personality disorder will only use you for as long as they can. They will then throw you away, and move on to their next target when they think you have nothing more to give. I wanted to see if he would treat me any better if he didn't know I was employed. Just as I suspected, he constantly rubbed it in my face that I didn't have a job, and he also laughed about how dumb I was for leaving. He told me that I better think the next time I decide to make a bone-headed decision to leave him.

While I was gone he didn't pay the mortgage or utilities for the entire 2 months. The house was going into pre-foreclosure. During our marriage counseling session with the therapist, my husband got angry because I would no longer lie for him, or cover for his bad behavior and the negative treatment I received from some of his family members. I told the therapist how he would seek out women with the same name as me and cheat with them. His explanation to me was so he wouldn't call me by the wrong name.

I explained that over the years I had put up with his lying, cheating, stealing, and immaturity but I was no longer going to put up with him choking and slamming me anytime he was mad with me, someone else, or mad that he would have to frequently change or empty his colostomy bag. He got angry and sat up from the couch to lunge towards me; the therapist said "No, no, no you won't do this in my office." I told her, "Now he is going to call me all kinds of bitches. He said, "No I'm not. Fuck you motherfucker and good luck catching up the motherfucking mortgage." As I said before, he thought he was leaving me in a financial rut with the mortgage because he didn't know I had my job back.

When I returned home, he told me that he borrowed money from his 401(k) retirement account. He said the purpose of withdrawing the money was so he could catch up and pay the mortgage. To my surprise, he didn't help me catch up the mortgage at all. I know I shouldn't have been surprised, but I always gave him the benefit of the doubt and trusted his word even when my gut intuition told me otherwise. Once again all of the financial burdens fell on my shoulders. After his outburst in the therapist's office I decided I needed to get protection.

He didn't hesitate to attempt to physically harm me in the presence of the therapist. I decided that day I needed to make a change. I knew I was going to be a dead woman if I was ever alone with him. The therapist's words kept resonating in my mind. There wouldn't be anyone to stop his rage or calm him down from finishing me off if I was alone with him. It didn't take much to set him off. When I returned home, I called my local women's shelter to set up an appointment to file for a Civil Protection Order.

After about a month or so after we separated, he must have become curious as to how I was surviving financially because I was still living in our family home. I believe he must have called the mortgage company because after numerous times of trying to contact the pastor who wouldn't answer the phone or return my calls, he finally called me back when the mortgage account became current and up-to-date.

The pastor pretended to be concerned and I say pretended because of his condescending tone of voice. He beat around the bush asking about my job situation, and what I planned on doing to have an income. During the height of the abuse, the pastor never told my husband he was wrong or to stop beating me. His advice to us was to stay in the relationship because he could see potential.

He never defined what "potential" meant. The only thing he told my husband was that we worked too hard to have a beautiful home and good jobs. He stressed to my husband that he didn't want to lose it all. Maybe that was his way of telling my husband to stop physically and verbally abusing me. My husband would call me different types of "bitches" in front of the pastor but the pastor wouldn't intervene. I even tried to explain some scenarios to the pastor in front of my abuser, so my abuser could hear from someone that he was wrong and it was not just my being sensitive or just my opinion.

My abuser in a calm and cool manner giggled with a slight laugh and said, "I don't know why you are telling the pastor because he can get it too. I don't care about what he says." The pastor seemed to be a bit nervous and didn't say much after that, and he didn't have any words of encouragement, chastisement, or even a prayer for that matter. I guess he didn't want to catch a beat down from a 6'1" 400lb man either.

By the grace of God, I was able to catch up the mortgage and continue to provide a home for me and my daughter. My husband wanted me to lose the house so he could then swoop in and take over the payments. He wanted to punish me by not paying the mortgage. His mission was to make sure I was out of the house for good. What he didn't know was that I had gotten my job back. My suspicions were in fact confirmed.

He wanted to punish me financially by not paying the back payments on the mortgage. This was apparent based on the demands in the divorce papers. See, here's the thing when you leave and come back it will only get worse. It gets worse because the abuser may feel as though he has lost complete control over you, he may be embarrassed that people have found out that you left, humiliated, and suffer an injury to his ego.

Once you leave you have to stay gone because it makes your abuser angrier, and he will seek to punish you by any means necessary. When you leave you draw people's attention, and your abuser will think that people think something is wrong with him because you left. Their fragile ego and insecurities can't handle such negative attention and outside judgments.

I stayed in my marriage because I loved my husband unconditionally and I respected the vows that I took before God. I didn't want to get a divorce. I submitted to my husband and revered him as the man of our home. He used this against me. He would tell me he knew I wouldn't leave because when we first met I told him I only wanted to get married once in my life. He also would tell me that he knew I would put up with his shit because I had put up with my mother's shit for so long. I sometimes wonder if he would have used the term "abuse" instead of "shit?" Would I have had the courage to seek help and get out sooner? I would do whatever it took to save my marriage. I never knew my life would depend on the survival of my marriage.

Your abuser may try to convince you that you are the problem. They may encourage you to go to counseling with a therapist or a pastor. The reality is, if your abuser has done this, he is not taking full responsibility for his abusive behavior. This is a manipulative tactic to keep you in the relationship. If he does not take responsibility for his abusive behavior towards you, the abusive behavior is not going to stop. He has to first acknowledge that you are not responsible for his actions. His abusive behavior towards you is a choice.

He needs to get professional help with his abusive behavior whether you choose to stay with him or not. It took me some time to understand that his abusive behavior is driven by power and control. You may be optimistic and hoping for him to change. You may want to believe him when he says he will change even if things don't feel different. You have to trust your instincts. If you don't feel safe, chances are, you are not safe.

If you are experiencing any of these things or even something similar that makes you uncomfortable, please contact the National Domestic Violence Hotline at 1-800-799-SAFE (7233) or visit www.NCADV.org. If you are being financially abused it makes it even more difficult to get out of an abusive relationship. You always want to make sure you have your own hidden money stash if any of these things are happening to you.

Divorce Court Abuse

One important piece of information I want to share with you is, don't be emotional in court. I know it is a lot easier said than done, but you must go to each court hearing with a poker face. Don't allow your abuser, his attorney, or the Guardian ad Litem to see you show any emotion. They are not your friends, advocates, or anyone who wants to support you by being fair. If you need to cry or be upset wait until you get home.

Don't do this in front of these individuals. My abuser's attorney would taunt me and make rude comments to try to bait me into a confrontation. He also made false accusations against me. Every time I would attempt to speak during court, his attorney would interrupt me or huff like an overgrown frustrated immature man child who was the bully of the playground.

You may feel relieved that someone outside of the home finally knows about the trauma you are going through. Don't make the mistake I made. I told the Guardian ad Litem about the years of abuse I had endured. It was embarrassing to tell, but I was afraid my abuser was finally going to kill me so I poured out my soul. I explained how my abuser would make our daughter say things or do things to me as a way to further abuse me.

❖ Speak Up & Get Out! ❖

When it was time to go back to court, the Guardian ad Litem completely slammed me in a written report as if I made everything up to make my abuser look bad. Luckily I had documentation from text messages from my abuser, emails, police reports, the report from the couples counseling, and social media posts to prove that I was telling the truth. Having these documents spoke volumes about his character and also proved to the Guardian ad Litem that I was not making these things up. I learned from my experience with my own mother to always have evidence to cover myself so no one can lie on me and get away with it.

A day after he was served with the Civil Protection Order, he went and filed for a divorce. I was completely blind-sided when I received the divorce papers. I couldn't understand why he didn't want to stop beating me. Why choose divorce? At the time I felt like divorce was worse than death. When the doorbell rang at our home, and the process server handed me the papers; my heart sank and my stomach dropped when I read them. Something inside of me knew what the documents were before I even opened the envelope.

I fell to the floor as I read the papers. I cried hysterically because at that moment I realized that there definitely was no turning back. There was no way to rewind time. No way to get back the pre-surgery husband. Some people say he was not worth my time prior to the surgery. So many people would say, "He is such an asshole." I would respond by saying, "Well, he's my asshole and I love him." I thought if I could just love him enough he would see my actions and know it. I still struggle with this because at least he was not beating me. Our relationship was not always bad. Now, I was faced with the reality that our relationship was over and our marriage was over. This was worse than death to me. This was the death of our marriage, our friendship, our companionship, our relationship, our hopes, our dreams, our goals, and our future together.

I went into the divorce process very naïve with no knowledge of the family court process or procedures. I thought we were going to be cordial with one another. I thought we could talk it out and maybe even possibly reconcile. I wanted to see a glimmer of the pre-surgery husband that I once knew. I couldn't help to wonder where the non-physically abusive man had gone. The man who showed up in divorce court was a mean, nasty, smirking, manipulative, cunning wordsmith, and downright rotten post-surgery husband that I didn't know. Not only did I have to be subjected to his taunts, but he had also hired a bullying unethical attorney that was a cloned combination of the pre-surgery and post-surgery husband that I had come to begin to know.

His attorney was like a jack of all trades and master of none. I am not an attorney, and I could clearly see that because this attorney was so focused on trying to intimidate me and bully me he made a lot of bad major decisions for my abuser in criminal and domestic court. Aside from his abrasive bullying behavior, I sometimes wondered if he knew he was supposed to be fighting for my abuser. Some of his decisions were clearly not in the favor of his client. The attorney also didn't have much wiggle room because each time they presented a lie or made an outrageous accusation, I always had documentation to prove them wrong. Be sure to keep very good records, keep them in a safe place, and document every single incident. Also formally file reports with the police or hospital.

Each time I attempted to speak in court his attorney would interrupt me, sigh, and make accusations to contradict my statements. This attorney was overly aggressive to the point where he made several bad decisions that didn't work out in the favor of my husband. It is not always wise to hire a pit bull type of an attorney that will take a bite and not let go. Often times these types of attorneys make inflammatory accusations to incite negative emotions in both parties. If you take the bait you will end up paying much more money than you anticipate because this behavior causes unnecessary delays in your case. His attorney wouldn't cooperate with my attorney. He would withhold documents or not submit requested documents in a timely manner.

Each time we went to divorce court we always had to request a new trial date because he and his attorney were missing documents, and we couldn't come to an agreement without the necessary documents. On the day our divorce was supposed to be finalized, we couldn't finalize the divorce because the list of items my attorney had requested from his attorney 3 months prior to this day had not been submitted by my husband or his attorney.

As a result, the list of items my abuser wanted out of the house was reviewed on this day as opposed to being reviewed, discussed, and agreed upon before this final date. We couldn't come to an agreement on the items which caused a delay in signing the final divorce papers in addition to the missing tax documents. His attorney was also notorious for showing up late for the court hearings, criminal court, as well as domestic court.

During what was supposed to be our final divorce court hearing, his attorney spent 2-3 hours of this day working on another case with another client in another room. I was billed by my attorney for the hours his attorney spent working with someone else. I was forced to sit there with my attorney, and wait for his attorney to finish working on an unrelated case. I asked my attorney if I was being billed by her for the time his attorney was spending on another case and her response was, "Yes".

I barely had the money to pay my attorney for the time she spent on my case, not to mention having to spend money for time that his attorney was spending on someone else's case. I had already used all of the funds from my retirement account which had dwindled down to almost nothing. To be honest, I had no clue where I was going to get the money from to finish paying for the divorce. I was frustrated because it was not fair for me to have to pay for time that was not being dedicated to our case.

By the time his attorney finished with the client on an unrelated case, the court was closing and had closed before we could sign the final papers for the divorce. A few weeks later I received a notice in the mail stating the next scheduled date for our divorce to be finalized was not for another 6 months. I immediately called my attorney's office because I didn't want to wait that long. It was just too painful emotionally. I told my attorney's secretary that he could have whatever he wanted, and I just wanted out at this point. I was completely hurt, broken, and tired. I had nothing left. My attorney contacted his attorney to say that I would just let him have everything but neither he nor his attorney responded back.

Make sure you have an attorney that will fight for you and has the best interest of you and your child. It is very important to hire an attorney that is familiar with domestic violence and the characteristics of abusers. If not, your attorney may be manipulated by your abuser. Your local women's shelter may be able to provide you with a list of local attorneys that are familiar with working on divorce cases that involve domestic violence and narcissistic abuse. No, we may not be a licensed therapist or counselor to diagnose someone with a personality disorder however, there is no mistaking our experience of abuse and the similarities of the abuser's characteristics, behaviors, and personality traits that are identical to what is described as narcissistic abuse. Never allow anyone to define your experience. You are the only one who has walked in your shoes.

Physical Abuse

Many people ask, "How did you let this happen?", "What did you do to make him beat you?", or "What did you say to him?" For a while I blamed myself and it was through the help of my local domestic violence women's shelter that I began to understand that I am not to blame. I want you to know that physical and verbal abuse is not about you; it is about the abuser's internal conflicts and struggles that they battle with and carry on a daily basis.

I didn't know emotional abuse and verbal abuse are just an introduction for physical abuse or even death. For some time I hid the dirty little secret of shame and embarrassment that this was happening to me. I would agree with everything my abuser said for fear of what he would say to me or do to me if I didn't agree, and not feeling good enough because he always found a way to make me feel bad.

After being choked, slammed, hit with objects, having a knife held to my throat & stomach, having knives thrown at me when he didn't get his way, and having sex so rough I would bleed and could barely walk afterwards. I had no other choice but to acknowledge all of the other forms of abuse I had endured over the years including the verbal, financial, and emotional abuse that I endured from some of his family members.

I guess deep down inside I knew he would eventually physically harm me because of how angry he would get over some of the smallest things. He would get so angry that he would throw things. Some days we could be laughing and having a great time, and out of nowhere he would insult me. Insult me to the point where it felt like he cut me to the white meat.

My abuser once grabbed me by my ear, and pinched very hard as we walked through the mall because he was upset that I spoke to a man and his woman partner. My abuser was upset because he didn't initially see the woman. It wasn't until he saw the woman that he let go of my ear. At the time I knew it hurt and my ear burned, but he was laughing the entire time as if he was joking. He would say, "You are mine woman, you better not be looking at no other man."

I once spoke to a group of women on the topic "*Know Your Worth and Change Your Life*", the following week my abuser beat me because I was called the following morning by another organization to speak. After he beat me, he said, "Now run and tell ya little women about that beat down." It was at that point that I no longer wanted to be a fraud. I began to speak up so I could get out of this painful situation. I no longer wanted to keep quiet.

I told the police, the prosecutor, family members, therapist, pastor, hospital, local domestic violence women's shelter, attorney, and other trusted individuals. I even wrote letters to the police and close friends stating that I wouldn't just leave without someone knowing where I was, I wouldn't leave my daughter, and if they found me dead from a suspicious looking death, to investigate my abuser and his father because my abuser had already tried to kill me and his father threatened to kill me. My abuser told the pastor that he would chop my head and put it so far back in the woods that no one would find me. I strongly suggest getting professional counseling. When I reported this threat to the prosecutor and the police they told me the pastor couldn't be subpoenaed to court because he is clergy.

Had he made this statement in front of a therapist or someone else, the statement could have been admissible in court. Once the physical abuse starts it does not stop. It only gets worse. Physical abuse can be devastating, painful, and life-changing. Physical abuse is a deliberate and intentional action that makes unwanted contact with another person.

Sometimes this contact will cause bleeding, bruising, broken bones, sprains, fractures, and/or pain. Other times depending on how clever your abuser is, they might deliberately not leave marks. My abuser took pride in how he could physically abuse me without leaving marks. Your best option if you are being physically abused is to SPEAK up and get out!

During the divorce, he would laugh at how he was living with his parents and no longer had any responsibilities for taking care of me, our home, and our daughter. I felt duped. I couldn't understand how I could love him unconditionally and be so loyal to him, and he could just turn his love for me off whenever he felt like it. I felt abnormal and even worse after I started being physically abused. Now, having to go through a messy, bitter, and painful divorce added on to the stress and pain of trying to cope with everything else.

I felt like I had been shaken in a snow globe and turned upside down. I can remember the first time he grabbed me by my throat and threw me across the room, all I could think was I just need to yell out for my pre-surgery husband to help me. I wanted my husband to come and stop this monster from attacking me. I felt so helpless because as I looked into his eyes, I didn't recognize who he had become. I had no one to protect me. In a flash, my prince charming turned into prince harming.

Below are just a few examples of what physical abuse can be:

- ¾ Spouse/partner putting their hands around your neck and strangling or choking you
- Being forced to have sex or sexual contact
- Biting

- Scratching
- Kicking
- Slapping
- Punching
- Poking you with their finger or an object
- Grabbing you by your clothing
- Holding a gun, knife, box cutter, bat, garden tool, or anything that can be used as a weapon against you
- Grabbing your breasts or hitting your butt aggressively
- Not allowing you to leave the home or force you to go someplace you don't want to go
- Throwing objects at you or in your direction
- Breaking your personal items
- Grabbing you by your hair
-

Social Media Abuse

Social Media abuse is the use of any electronic device that can be used for sending emails, text messages, or the ability to post bullying, intimidating, humiliating, harassing messages or technological stalking behavior on a public social platform such as Facebook, Twitter, Instagram, etc…. Social Media abuse is a form of emotional and verbal abuse.

My abuser became extremely mean and miserable after the initial surgery that turned our lives upside down. He was very gifted at writing poetry. Poetry seemed to be his first love. Poetry came natural to him. I had started journaling years ago as a result of hearing Oprah talk about how therapeutic and liberating journaling and writing can be. I noticed my abuser no longer had the motivation to do anything. He wouldn't take his medication unless I gave it to him, he wouldn't shower or bathe unless I helped him, and he wouldn't drink his protein shakes unless I made them.

He didn't want to be bothered with anyone, and he seemed to be losing all hope as if life was over.

As a way to encourage him, I purchased a brand new notebook for him that had inspirational quotes and surprised him with it. I told him here's to a fresh start to write some poetry to get his mind off of the horrible surgeries, and all of the fears he had surrounding the next surgery he was going to have. He threw the notebook across the room, called me a dumb ass bitch, and said he didn't have a desire to write poetry anymore.

He said he no longer had it in him. He said the old him died along with everything else, and the old him was dead never to come back. He told me not to expect him to laugh anymore, write poetry, or do any of that dumb shit we used to do. I felt sorry for him and helpless because nothing I did to try to ease his pain made him happy. If anything it seemed to have made him dislike me even more.

Once I filed for the Civil Protection Order, he was no longer permitted to contact me directly. He would always tell me that he knew me better than I knew myself. While I was gone after fleeing in the middle of the night, he would post love and relationship related messages and poetry. When I came back he asked me if I saw them. I joked with him and said, "No." Then we both laughed and agreed at the same time that I looked. He told me he knew I was looking, so he posted something every chance he could get so I would see it.

He said that was exactly why he was posting because he wanted me to know that he was sorry for what he had done. I asked him why he would be so mean on the phone and he immediately got angry, and said it was because I hurt his feelings by leaving and he was mad at me. He wanted me to hurt the same way he was hurting.

I don't know why, but once we separated I was in shock to see that he consistently posted mean, hateful, threatening, and defamatory messages on social media about me in the form of poetry. I couldn't believe my eyes! I also couldn't believe the number of people he had fooled into believing that he was this poor little innocent victim who had done nothing wrong.

When I spoke to his best friend's widow she said she would read the posts and automatically knew he was referring to me. She said, "He wrote everything except your name, but we all knew who he was talking about. "I would get messages from other people asking me if he knew that his daughter would someday grow up, and read these messages that he posted about his wife and her mother?"

He seemed to have gained a lot of women by playing the, "I am sick and separated from my wife...see look at my wounds (literally and figuratively)," card. He made it seem as though I was this horrible wife that no longer loved him or wanted him. It frustrated me because once again he was not telling the truth, and he was lying and manipulating others to get his way. I finally had to tell myself if he got over on me for so many years and reeled me in with his charm and deep dimples, how can I be upset with these people who believe his cruel messages and social media posts?

Abusers are duplicate people. They portray themselves to be a nice guy to others and save their abusive self for you and your children behind closed doors. These abusers are also master manipulators. Since others have not witnessed or experienced their abuse, it is easy for them to be manipulated and believe whatever the abuser says to be true. Abusers will play the "poor me" card to get sympathy from others.

They will also befriend or begin to hang out with family or friends that they previously criticized, and didn't want you to interact with. Some of these people will believe the abuser and join in on the emotional abuse, others will remain silent, and some will show sporadic support. Those who show sporadic support for you are afraid your abuser will find out they are supporting you. They are fearful of your abuser treating them the way he has treated you. These interactions and alliances can be formed either in person or via social media.

My abuser talked very poorly about some of his family members, and didn't want me to spend time with them. I finally figured out the reason for this. If you have all of the players that you are manipulating talking to each other, it is much harder to divide and conquer them. It is much more difficult to make people dislike one another if they know each other firsthand, have direct contact, and direct communication with one another.

This explains why he would tell me that someone said something negative about me, but he never wanted me to address them directly. So the next time I would see the person, I was not my usual friendly self. This made me look bad because I have now put two and two together to understand that the person may not have said anything bad about me at all. This was just his way to prevent me from bonding with some of his family members and creating a good solid relationship. I look back and I have so many a-ha moments where I realize just how clever, manipulative, and cunning this man really was. I now understand why his female cousin seemed to have an issue with me every time I turned around. It was the result of something he drummed with her about me. Everyone he said he didn't like, are the people he friended on social media. He began to call all of the women on social media affectionate names. These were the same names he would call me in the beginning of our relationship when he was love-bombing me.

Here are some examples of Social Media Abuse.

- Your abuser may send you private or direct messages to force you to respond to something he has posted.
- Dictates who you can be connected with online
- Monitors your online activity to see when you are online or last time you were active online
- Publicly humiliates you in his social media post updates
- Demands your passwords to all of your accounts
- Questions your list of followers or friends
- Checks your phone and messages on a regular basis to see who you have been communicating with
- Punishes you if you don't respond immediately to his messages

The following is an example of one of the posts that my abuser posted on social media the day after the court ordered him to pay child support for our daughter. The name and photo of his eyes have been removed for privacy purposes. He posted a close-up of his eyes as a way to intimidate me back into silence. As you will see there is also a play on words with my name because he and others call me "Meek" which is short for Tamika. This post was one of over one hundred posts that he had posted to social media. This post was also admissible in criminal court and used as evidence to prosecute my abuser in the criminal domestic violence case. This is why I stress the importance of saving information and documenting everything.

> Ngha Umma Beast wild eye'd free! As long as air fills my lungs Umma problem son or should I say daughter- The attempt to pimp me like a hooker on the street; twisted. Shiiiit... I was the King warming between yo sheets making sure yo ass could eat.... I speak truth between beats to truth seekers and the only Ngha's that matter While your lies reach inside dead minds With each lie you tweak. Each lie you freak gives you solace as you feed the ignorance of the meek....

Once I filed for a civil protection order, social media became my abuser's new weapon of choice to further abuse me once he was no longer permitted to contact me directly. I suffered public humiliation through his defaming social media posts and messages. He used to tell me over the years how he studied me and knew me better than I knew myself. He would say, "I know what you are going to do before you do it."

When I finally got a backbone and got the courage to speak up to him and some of his family members it threw him off balance. Since he could no longer contact me, he knew me well enough to know that if he posted something on social media I would see it. What he didn't take into consideration is that I was not the only set of eyes watching. God know and sees all. I was in so much pain and I would cry out to God to help me, and stop him from lying on me. I had given this man my all and none of it mattered to him.

This tactic is referred to as Baiting and Bashing. Abusers enjoy playing this game. Their goal is to provoke you into trying to defend yourself publicly. The purpose of this is to make you appear mentally unstable or that everything is your fault. An abuser does not like to take responsibility. He will divert the attention away from himself and onto you. He is a bully who seeks the support of others to carry out his attacks on you.

This is extremely catastrophic for someone who has already endured his abuse privately. The abuser knows you are already suffering from their mistreatment, blame, abuse, slander, rejection, and isolation. They want to see you shattered into a million pieces. An abuser delights in this. You may already know the familiar smirk I am referring to.

The abuser gets a certain level of satisfaction knowing you are being tormented by the social media posts. He basks in the positive and sympathetic attention he gets from the people he has tricked into believing he is an innocent victim. The intent of this is to not only demean his victim, but to also scare her into not speaking up and telling the truth about who he really is.

Each day he would post derogatory messages disguised as poetry on multiple social media websites. The posts were a part of a character assassination smear campaign on me as well as his way of trying to intimidate me and keep me from testifying. Some of the messages were so scary and disturbing; I printed them out and gave them to the prosecutor and judge.

They were used as evidence in the domestic violence case. The judge read the messages, and determined they were messages of intimidation and threats on my life. The other messages were used in the domestic divorce court as evidence to speak about his character and his level of maturity in regards to him wanting custody of our daughter.

Everyone that he said he hated and didn't want me to talk to because they had done something horribly wrong or hurtful to him was now his "friend" or "follower" on social media. Every ex-girlfriend that he had in the past became his ally via social media. Every type of woman that he claimed he would never date because he hated their race is the type of women he preyed on. He also preyed on women who were educated or had a substantial income as a means to sustain the lifestyle I had provided for him.

He once told our daughter, "Hey, if your mom was a busted bitch working for $8.50 an hour at the bank, I wouldn't be with her ass." Each day I woke up and in the middle of the night I couldn't resist looking to see what he was going to post next, and it was so painful. I knew it was painful, and it was getting worse by the day. It was like the old saying goes, I was pouring salt in an open wound and not allowing it to heal. Looking at those posts each day was like peeling the scab off of a wound that was trying to heal.

A part of me continued this pattern because I thought that somewhere inside of him he would be remorseful and post a cryptic message of a half assed apology. Something to say he was sorry for all of the things he had done to me. I never got that, just like I didn't get why I was so foolishly loyal to him to a fault.

I couldn't believe the lies he was posting about me on Social Media. I couldn't believe how he portrayed himself as an innocent victim. I couldn't believe how he turned on me and acted as though I was his worst enemy. I wanted to sleep through the pain. I wanted to sleep through the court dates of the criminal domestic violence case and the divorce court hearings. I even wanted to sleep through my therapy sessions because I didn't want to face the painful truth that I was living a life that I no longer recognized.

He and his attorney used a dirty tactic in the beginning of the divorce accusing me of trying to commit suicide. They made this claim right after I filed for a civil protection order, so he could gain full custody of our daughter. The purpose was to make me look insane and like an unfit mother. The reality is when he went on his social media smear campaign; I was closer to suicide than I had ever thought of being in my entire life.

However, I cried and I screamed, and I begged God to hear me, to feel my pain, to see that what he was doing to me was wrong. He turned people against me that didn't even know me or our story. I was hurt, broken, and feeling dejected as I began to wrap my brain around the crushing realization that I loved a fictional character. I loved someone who never existed. This was almost too much to bear. The agony of being isolated and voiceless is a nightmare that is indescribable. I didn't get to sleep through my painful journey, click skip, or press fast forward and neither will you. But you will get through the painful process you are going through. It takes time and faith.

I was in a very dark place during the domestic violence and divorce court hearings process. It was like he and his attorney were doing everything they knew how to push me over the edge emotionally. He would even post messages on social media with hashtags that said, "Kill yo-self." I was losing everything; I had lost my husband, family, job, and even myself. I had to face the painful truth that I was almost forty years old having to start my life over from scratch. He was slandering me on social media and in the real world.

I had already experienced this with my own mother going on her own smear campaign about me. I will tell you, abusers don't like it when you speak up for yourself and create boundaries. The hurtful part was that he would get upset when people treated me badly because of something my abusive mother had said about me. He didn't like when someone would treat me badly or judge me based on the lies my mother told people about me.

However, he turned around and did the same thing to me as my abusive mother had done for years and even to the present day. He knew exactly how to hurt me because I had poured my heart out to him about how my mother had treated me as a child growing up. He even witnessed her abusive behavior towards me on different occasions. He even wanted to call her or go to her house and cuss her out. I wouldn't allow him to do so because after all she did birth me. I was so busy running from an abusive childhood that followed me into my adulthood; I ended up trading a witch for the devil. It was like jumping out of the frying pan directly into the fire.

My abuser slandered me on various social media platforms, and I wanted so badly to defend myself. I prayed and cried out to God to help me. A still small voice spoke to me and said, "Be quiet, don't defend yourself, and don't be concerned with your reputation. I will silence your enemies." It was a struggle watching day after day being slandered through poetry on social media.

The lesson I learned was not to bother defending myself to people who care nothing about me. People are going to talk about you no matter what. Don't let it shake you. I have even learned to own my shortcomings and mistakes before someone can use them against me. This is how my business was birthed. When my friend said she was going to out me as a fraud because my husband was beating me, and she felt like I shouldn't be talking to women about knowing their worth. I immediately found a way to incorporate my journey of surviving abuse into my business. Let's face it, no one can tell your story better than you can.

If you are being abused through social media don't worry about what other people say about you. Yes, it is painful and you will want to defend yourself. Your abuser will eventually expose who he really is to the public. Some people will know he is wrong but they won't say anything to him because they already know what he is capable of doing. Why, because they see how he publicly humiliates you. Most people don't want your abuser to treat them the way they see him treating you. Therefore, they don't get involved.

I had people to tell me to stop looking at his social media pages. They were giving the best advice they knew how at the time. Each situation is unique. I didn't listen. Although viewing the posts was a painful thing to do; I was able to print the posts and use them in court to show evidence of his character and what he was capable of saying and doing. These posts spoke volumes to his character. The social media posts showed a different side of him that he didn't present during our court appearances. These social media posts were admissible in court, and contributed to his conviction of criminal domestic violence.

If you are experiencing any of these things or something similar you are not to blame. You are not responsible for your spouse's or partner's behavior. You are also not alone. Domestic abuse transcends race, education, socioeconomic status, age, and religion.

CHAPTER 3

Warning Signs: Is That Right? Did He Really Do That?

"You have the gift of a brilliant internal guardian that stands ready to warn you of hazards and guide you through risky situations." ~Gavin de Becker

---

Now I want to share with you some of the red flags and warning signs that I experienced firsthand during my relationship and marriage. I've also included the "Signs to look for in a Battering Personality" courtesy of Project for Victims of Family Violence, Fayetteville, AR. They outline 17 different forms of behaviors that are accurate indicators of an abuser.

1. **Possessiveness:** At the beginning of a relationship, an abuser may say that jealousy (actually possessiveness) is a sign of love. Possessiveness has nothing to do with love. It is a sign of having a lack of trust. The abuser may question his partner about who she talks to, accuse her of flirting, or keep her from spending time with family, friends, or children. As the possessiveness progresses, he may call her frequently during the day or drop by unexpectedly. He may refuse to let her work for fear she'll meet someone else. He may even engage in behaviors like checking her car mileage or asking friends to watch her.

2. **Controlling Behavior:** At first, the batterer will say this behavior is due to his concern for her safety, her need to use her time well, or her need to make good decisions. He will be angry if the woman is "late" coming

back from the store or an appointment. He will question her closely about where she went and who she talked with. As this behavior progresses, he may not let the woman make personal decisions about the house, her clothing, or even going to church. He may keep all the money or even make her ask permission to leave the house or room.

3. **Quick Involvement:** Many battered women dated or knew their abuser for less than six months before they were married, engaged, or lived together. He comes in like a whirlwind, claiming, "You're the only person I could ever talk to" or "I've never been loved like this by anyone." He will pressure the woman to commit to the relationship. Later, the woman may feel very guilty or that she's "letting him down" if she wants to slow down involvement or break off the relationship.

4. **Unrealistic Expectations:** Abusive men will expect their partner to meet all their needs. He expects a perfect wife, mother, lover, and friend. He'll say things like, "If you love me, I'm all you need, and you're all I need." He expects his partner to take care of everything for him emotionally and in the home.

5. **Isolation:** The abusive person tries to cut his partner off from all resources. If she has male friends, she's a "whore." If she has women friends, she's a lesbian. If she's close to family, she's "tied to the apron strings." He accuses those who support the woman of causing trouble. He may want to live in the country, without a telephone, or refuse to let her drive the car. He may try to keep her from working or going to school.

6. **Blames Others For Problems:** If he is chronically unemployed, someone is always "doing him wrong" or "out to get him." He may make mistakes and then blame the woman for upsetting him and keeping him from concentrating on the task. He may tell the woman she is at fault for virtually anything that goes wrong in his life.

7. **Blames Others For Feelings:** The abuser may tell his partner "You make me mad," or "You're hurting me by not doing what I want you to do," or "I can't help being angry." He's the one who makes the decision about

what he thinks or feels, but he will use these feelings to manipulate his partner. Harder to catch are claims, "You make me happy," or "You control how I feel."

8. **Hypersensitivity:** An abuser is easily insulted. He claims his feelings are hurt, when in fact he is angry or is taking the slightest setback as a personal attack. He will rant and rave about the injustice of things that have happened, things that are just a part of living. These include being asked to work late, getting a traffic ticket, being asked to help with chores, or being told some behavior is annoying.

9. **Cruelty To Animals Or Children:** Abusers may punish animals brutally or be insensitive to their pain or suffering. An abuser may expect children to be capable of things beyond their abilities. For example, he may punish a 2 year old for wetting a diaper. Or he might tease children until they cry. Some studies indicate that about 60% of men who physically abuse their partners also abuse their children.

10. **Sexual Abuse:** An abuser may physically assault private parts of a woman's body without any concern about whether she wants to have sex or not. He might use violence to coerce her into sexual activities or he may begin having sex with her while she's asleep. He may force her to perform sexual acts that she finds uncomfortable, unpleasant, or degrading. He may demand sex after he physically beats her.

11. **Verbal Abuse:** His language is intentionally meant to be cruel and hurtful. Through verbal abuse he degrades his partner and belittles her accomplishments. The abuser often tells her she's stupid and unable to function without him. He may wake her up to verbally abuse her and to prevent her from sleeping.

12. **Rigid Sex Roles:** The abuser expects his partner to serve him. He may even say the woman must stay at home and obey in all things - even acts that are criminal in nature. The abuser sees women as inferior to men, responsible for menial tasks, and unable to be a whole person without a relationship.

13. **Dr. Jekyll/Mr. Hyde Personality:** Many women are confused by the abuser's sudden changes in mood. She may think he has some sort of

mental problem because one minute he's agreeable, the next he's explosive. Explosiveness and moodiness are typical of men who beat their partners. These behaviors are related to other characteristics, such as hypersensitivity.

14. Past Battering: The abuser may say he has hit women in the past, but blame them for the abuse. He might say, "They made me do it" or "She deserved it, you don't know her mouth." Relatives or ex-partners may tell the woman that he is abusive and controlling. A batterer will abuse any woman he is with if the relationship lasts long enough for the violence to begin. Situational circumstances don't make anyone's personality abusive.

15. Threats of Violence: This includes any threat of physical force meant to control the partner. This includes statements like, "I'll slap your mouth off," "I'll kill you," and "I'll break your neck." Most people don't threaten their partners. Abusers will try to excuse their threats by saying that everybody talks that way. No, everybody does not talk that way.

16. Breaking or Striking Objects: Breaking a woman's possessions is used as a punishment. Primarily, it's used to terrorize the woman into submission. The abuser may beat on the table with his fist, or throw objects around or near his partner. There is great danger when someone thinks he has the right to punish or frighten his partner.

17. Any Force During an Argument: This may involve the abuser holding the woman down, physically restraining her from leaving the room or the residence, or any pushing, poking, or shoving. He may hold his partner against the wall or pin her down on the floor telling her, "You're going to listen to me."

I was puzzled about why I felt like I no longer knew myself. I used to be confident, outgoing, and decisive. In this relationship I gradually became passive, submissive, and indecisive. I also lowered my standards in various areas of my life. I felt lost.

I have always been the kind of person to bounce back quickly from adversity. I would stand my ground and voice my opinion. Unfortunately, in this relationship I found myself spiraling deeper and deeper into a black hole of despair and depression. I couldn't bounce back emotionally. I knew something was wrong. I was unable to regain my confidence and live fully in my purpose. I watched my goals and dreams slowly fade away. I didn't want to offend him or make him feel bad so I started turning down promotions and opportunities. I did this to avoid his negative comments.

Initially, he was very supportive of me. He was my biggest cheerleader. He encouraged me to get my doctorate. He was like my education pimp. Even after I got my doctorate he wanted me to go back to school to become an attorney. Over time, his attitude towards me changed rapidly. The trauma was like nothing I had ever experienced. I constantly questioned myself. Why could I not heal from the pain of being used and abused? Why didn't I have the courage to say, "Enough is enough" and reach out for help, or say, "No?" Why didn't I have any boundaries?

Below are some personality types, characteristics, and tactics of abusers. If you are experiencing any of these, you are more than likely the victim of domestic violence and narcissistic abuse.

Narcissistic Personality Disorder

Narcissistic Personality Disorder or (NPD) can be described as:

- Needs constant attention and praise
- Lacks empathy towards others
- Needs to be the center of attention
- Arrogant
- Takes advantage of others
- Has a sense of entitlement
- Lacks respect for other's feelings or wishes
- Does not have boundaries in regards to others
- Envious of others accomplishments or achievements
- A Pathological liar (lies about anything and everything)
- Needs constant affirmation from others

- Manipulative
- Believes he is special, invincible, or a superhero
- Believes he is above everyone else
- Believes others are beneath him
- Puts others down to make himself feel better

A Narcissist will live a secret life that you don't know about. They have dual personalities. They will be nice in public and a hell-raiser behind closed doors. They cause severe trauma to their spouse and children.

Narcissistic Abuse

Narcissistic Abuse is extremely damaging. It's much more difficult to recover from narcissistic Abuse. It's like no other abuse. Recovering from this type of abuse is not a "normal" recovery from abuse. This type of abuse causes erosive damage to the person being abused. Some narcissists are violent and some are not. However, they are very controlling. One of the ways they're able to control their temper is by controlling you, playing crazy making head games to keep you off balance. This makes you unable to speak up for yourself when you know you should.

The moment they're no longer able to control you, or feel like they're losing control over you is when you will catch the wrath of their narcissistic rage. Anything can trigger a spontaneous out of control violent rage from a narcissist. Take every precaution you can to be safe and remain safe if your abuser has threatened your life or told you, "If he can't have you, no one else can." This is not just a cliché line abusers like to use.

Narcissistic Rage

You will feel the wrath of a narcissist when he unexpectedly explodes at you over something minor. When he finally calms down long enough you'll learn that he had built up this anger towards you over a long time. You will learn that he didn't like you, was jealous of you, at some point he was even offended by you. Then "BOOM!" it all comes rushing out at once into a violent rage. You may have even asked him at some point if he's okay, or if you have offended him. He may have responded in a calm and cool manner that he wasn't offended. In fact he really was offended. Narcissists are passive-aggressive people. In situations where most people are angry or upset, a narcissist will be cooler than a cucumber.

I would always say, "Wow, you have the patience of Job! Aren't you upset?" The answer would always be a disturbing "No" no matter what the situation was, or how upsetting it was, or who was involved. Understand this, a narcissist is not letting things slide. You are not off the hook. Narcissists keep mental notes on how they will get revenge on the person who injured their ego or who they feel has wronged them. Narcissistic rage also occurs when the abuser feels like he's losing power and control over you. He needs to physically abuse you to beat you back into submission.

Narcissistic Supply

Narcissistic supply is the attention a narcissist seeks from others. In order to function, he needs constant praise, affirmation, and attention. There has to be a constant flow of compliments and validation. You are not permitted to disagree with or challenge a narcissist if he views you as supply. If you do disagree with a Narcissist or assert yourself, you will experience his narcissistic rage.

A narcissist will seek to gain attention from family, friends, social media followers or friends, or any other source that will distract him. This attention will keep him from facing his own personal shortcomings, insecurities, and fragile ego.

A narcissist will always have back-up supply to shower him with an over abundance of attention if you decide to build up the courage to go against his beliefs. The moment he no longer receives constant praise and admiration from his spouse, children, or main source of supply, he will discard them as if they never existed. You will become public enemy number one. You will be nothing more than yesterday's trash to him.

Gaslighting

I learned this term when I was at the prosecutor's office during the preliminary phase of filing a criminal charge for domestic violence. I was explained to the prosecutor that since my husband had been gone from our home; I no longer misplaced important documents, mail, rolls of 100 postage stamps, or lost my personal items around the house. Since he left, if I did misplace something I found it almost immediately or did a quick back track.

When my abuser was around items such as lip gloss, receipts, rolls of postage stamps, important mail or documents would disappear never to be found again. When I asked him if he had seen any of these items on different occasions, he would get agitated or tell me I never purchased something or never had something when I knew I did.

I began to question myself, and I thought my severe headaches were beginning to affect my memory. The prosecutor immediately explained to me that this term comes from the 1940's movie *Gaslighting*. She told me that this is a common tactic abusers use on their victims. The goal of the abuser when using this technique is to cause the victim to question her reality, her memory, and how she perceives things, and her overall sanity. Gaslighting gradually erodes your self-confidence, your ability to focus, and makes you question your ability to make major and minor decisions. Ultimately, your abuser wants to render you helpless so you will become dependent only on him.

The main reason I began recording our telephone conversations after he began physically abusing me; is because he would tell the pastor I said something I didn't say, say I didn't say something I did say, or he wouldn't admit to saying something very mean and cruel to me. He would tell me that an event didn't occur the way I described, and that I was being sensitive, playing the victim, or blowing things out of proportion. I began to question my sanity, and I questioned my memory. Whenever he spoke, he expected me to listen attentively with no reaction. The moment I would begin to share my point of view he would suck his teeth, roll his eyes, or interrupt me yelling, "I call BULLSHIT" as if my opinion didn't matter. Every time I asked him why he rolled his eyes, he always insisted that he didn't know how to roll his eyes and that I was imagining things.

Enduring and overcoming abuse is tough enough. However, trying to recover from narcissistic abuse is even tougher. There are 3 stages that a narcissistic abuser will take you through during your time with him. There is no set time frame. It may take 1 month, 6months, 1 year, or 30 years for him to get through all of these stages.

Multiple factors play a part in the timeframe. He could be bored with you, you may no longer have what he wants or needs, or he may see a shinier object and you no longer fit into his mold. The first stage is idealization, the second stage is devaluing, and the third stage is discarding. I also included love bombing because it plays a vital role in winning you over in the idealization phase.

Idealization

In this stage when you first meet him, he is very loving, kind, romantic, attentive, and charming. He will profess his love for you. He will tell you how you possess all of the qualities he is looking for in a woman. He will tell you how you are so much better than his exes or other women. You understand him better than anyone else. He will also tell you how his exes cheated on him and how they are all crazy. He is telling you about them cheating on him as a way to let you know that if you want to keep him you better not do the same. It also places you into the position of wanting to please him.

You want to show him that you are nothing like his exes. So you begin to prove to him that you will love him, care for him, never cheat on him, or do any of the things to him that his exes had done. If he has not yet left the relationship or he is in the process of moving on. He will tell you all about how awful his ex has treated him. He'll tell you she's abusive, uses him, and has no compassion for him. He'll tell you all about how he tried to save his failing relationship but because of her issues he just couldn't save the relationship. He'll say all of the right things to make you fall madly in love with him. He offers non-stop flow of compliments that make you feel as though you are the most beautiful woman in the world. He will even downplay your known visible flaws and you will be on a natural high. These tactics are called love bombing.

Love Bombing

Love bombing usually occurs in the beginning when you first meet your abuser. If you're everything that an abuser wishes he could be or you have what the abuser wishes he had you will instantaneously become his prey. He will do anything and everything he can to pull you into a relationship with him, then immediately begin to brainwash and control you in very subtle ways. He'll smother and overwhelm you with kind acts.

During this phase he'll test your boundaries by doing something offensive to you just to see how you will react. Each time he'll push the envelope a little further until you have absolutely no boundaries with him. He will quickly follow-up with overbearing kindness so that you will excuse his bad behavior. This is a huge red flag. *If he doesn't respect your boundaries he won't respect you.*

This is a recipe for disaster later in the relationship if you pursue a future with this man. The act of love bombing consists of going overboard with love, attention, compliments, gifts, affection, excessive phone calls, countless text messages each day, showing up to your home or job unexpectedly, and monitoring your online activity. If you are not answering his phone calls or text messages and he immediately contacts you through social media to let you know he can see your online status, this is a red flag. This is *very* unhealthy behavior.

Early in a relationship, we often don't see anything wrong with these actions. We're flattered by all of the attention he gives us. We may have even previously experienced abuse, and if we didn't heal properly from that relationship; we may feel completely ecstatic that someone is drowning us in compliments.

In my situation, my abuser later told me that he studied me. That is exactly what abusers do in the beginning. They study you to know your likes, dislikes, and to know exactly what to tell you or promise you in order to gain control. They may ask you non-stop questions as a way to make you think they are highly interested in you. They also just allow you to talk and pour your heart out to them. This is a very deliberate method that abusers use to take mental notes on exactly how to control and manipulate you later on in the relationship.

They also test you by pushing the envelope to see how far they can go with crossing your boundaries. If he does something rude or says something that makes you uncomfortable, you need to address it. You can't ignore it. Once you've clearly addressed the issue with him, if he continues the same behavior that makes you uncomfortable, this is a red flag.

He may even agree that he was wrong, so that he can smooth over the situation to take your mind off of the issue. He has no intentions of respecting your wishes or boundaries. You'll realize this when you find yourself addressing the same issue more than once. All of the attention he gives you is a distraction to keep you from trying to get to know who he really is. You may even be flattered by what I call, "Mr. Me Too".

Mr. Me Too will claim to have the same goals, vision, favorite color, likes, and dislikes as you. Any interests you have, you can rest assure he has the same identical interests. This is not real. He will want to spend all of his time with you. He will want to be by your side all of the time. He will soon become so overbearing that you no longer have time for friends or family. You won't even have time to focus on goals you may have set for yourself. The only way you will accomplish your goals is if he sees a way that he can directly benefit from the results.

Your life will revolve around him and making sure his needs are met.

I reached the point where I was downright exhausted. I felt like I was the only one on the basketball court running back and forth making all of the baskets, putting in the hard work, and running myself raggedy. Meanwhile, he sat on the sidelines in the bleachers eating, watching, and waiting to reap the benefits with a cheer here and there to make sure I didn't quit and give up.

He also beat me because he was angry that my business was not making the kind of money he thought it should have been making at the time. He said that he should be sitting on the beach sipping on his drink. He wanted me to make money but at the same time he didn't want me to book speaking engagements and be in the spotlight. I tried to explain to him that I couldn't generate the kind of money he wanted because I had gotten sick, his parents had gotten sick, he got sick and then our daughter had her spinal fusion surgery months after his first initial surgery.

He was discharged from the hospital on a Tuesday and our daughter went in for an 8 hour surgery on that Friday. I was taking care of everyone's medical documents, talking to the doctors and making sure everything and everyone was okay. I was barely keeping my head above water physically. I was exhausted. I made up my mind that at this point, my business was not a priority. My priority was making sure everyone regained their health.

He may also want to spend hours on the phone if he can't physically be with you. If he's not with you and can't be on the phone with you he may constantly instant message you asking you what you're doing. He will try to convince you that you two are soulmates and that he has never loved anyone as much as he loves you. You may also hear all about how no one understands him the way you do. This is not real. He's only pretending to be someone he's not, just to gain control over you and what you may have to offer that will benefit him.

When he can't fulfill the lies and promises he has told you, the nice loving kind man will begin to rapidly fade away. Over time he will get tired of pretending to be someone he's not You will begin to see glimpses of who he really is and when he completely unravels, you will experience who he truly is. I can assure you this won't be a good experience either.

In the beginning my abuser told me he was the male version of me because we had so much in common. I must admit I was in awe at how much we had in common. Looking back, he let me do all of the talking. I now realize that he was just feeding off of my words. At the time I was majoring in Psychology and I wanted to own my own practice someday. Guess what? He did too. The surprising part is that he wasn't even enrolled in school. Years had gone by and he always stuck to this story but never did anything to move toward accomplishing this goal.

When we first met, called me countless times during the day and paged me just as many times. He would send me flowers, take me to dinner, and he would drive 2 hours to show up at my house without calling on numerous occasions. When he was getting ready to leave for the military, he gave me a teddy bear, my favorite candy bar, Hershey's hugs and kisses, and a plastic toy sword. This is about the most romantic thing I had experienced at the time. He told me when he was gone to do the following things: when I get lonely and miss him to hold the bear as a representation of him, eat a Hershey's Hug when I needed a hug from him, eat a Hershey's kiss if I needed a kiss from him, when I needed protection the little plastic toy sword would protect me, and if I ever felt low in my spirits from missing him, eat my favorite candy bar to boost my mood and energy.

WOW! Now that was some strong game especially for a young naive 19 year old girl. Every time he came in town to see me, he always brought flowers and a lovely handwritten poem that would melt my heart each and every time. It made me forget about the times he would disappear for days or not answer my calls to him. It also made me forget about all of the times I would ask him to stop swearing in front of my parents, or all of the other red flags that I ignored.

Devalue

After he has won you over through the use of idealization and love-bombing you are at risk for entering the devaluing stage. During this stage he will begin to get tired of you. You may no longer serve a purpose for him as he gets bored very easily. This can happen instantaneously. Especially if he feels you will never go anywhere or leave him. The thrill of trying to keep you is gone. He will become cold, rude, unloving, and give you the silent treatment. You may begin to feel as though you no longer exist in his life.

The person who once accepted you, your flaws, and everything about you now hates everything about you. He will use information against you that you previously confided in him about. Everything he said his exes had done to him, are now the things he accuses you of doing. He constantly checks your phone, text messages, and emails. You once thought you could laugh and talk about anything. Now he becomes irate and takes everything personal as if you said something to insult him or you have some hidden meaning behind what you say. He becomes paranoid and accuses you of being his enemy. He will also look into your eyes and make promises he has no intentions of keeping. He will lie to you without hesitation.

In the stage of devaluing you, he may treat you perfectly fine in public yet behind closed doors he abuses you in some way. You will be confused not knowing how someone can go from hot to cold in a split moment. If you begin to withdraw from him by not showering him with compliments and constant praise, he will begin to seek out a new source of supply. He will turn on you. You will become his number 1 enemy. Nothing you do will ever be good enough for him.

He will still continue to string you along and he will cheat on you and have affairs with other women or men. He will get great satisfaction in knowing that he is able to lie to you and cheat on you and practically get away with it. If you find out about the cheating he will lie about it, laugh about it, and fly into a rage because you are questioning his reckless behavior. My abuser once told me that he got fat to prove to me that he was not cheating on me. That was a lie because he had several women on the side.

The source of supply can be his family members, friends, exes, new women, or a child he previously discarded. He won't choose the new women based on love interest. These women will be chosen based on what he can get from them (sex, money, status etc…) and how well he can manipulate them. They may be a single mom, coming out of an abusive relationship, or known to have been in an abusive relationship. Or a woman with a good income, or an education, or pursuing an education that will lead to a good career. Ultimately he will use them for status or something benefits him.

He will portray himself as a victim of his ex or soon-to-be ex, and position himself to be the perfect gentlemen who will be their knight in shining armor. He always tried to use the method of triangulation (which we will discuss in a moment) to make me jealous of other women. He would get angry because I refused to confront other women about him. I blamed him, not the women. For all I knew, they may not have known he was married.

As a way to try to keep him, you will go into a major people pleasing mode with him. You will do everything you can to keep him from getting angry or flying into an uncontrollable rage. He will blame you for everything. The once great sex life you shared will be rare to non-existent. That too will be a faded memory. The passionate kisses, late night pillow talks, dinner dates, and all of the romantic things he used to do for you are nothing but faded memories. The only time you will experience a glimpse of this is if he senses that you are thinking about leaving him or that you are gaining a sense of independence. He will be nice long enough to keep you from leaving him.

Discarding

In the third and final stage, you mean absolutely nothing to your abuser. He is completely finished with you, and if he has not already, he has thrown you away as if you are meaningless trash. Once you have reached this point with a narcissist there is no going back or compromising. Sometimes he will gradually get to this point and other times you will be completely blindsided. You won't or didn't see it coming. In this phase, you will discover that your abuser has been planning to dump you for some time.

He is just waiting for the perfect opportunity. He has already slandered you to other people and already has his new love interest lined up. His purpose of slandering you is strategically planned. The purpose is to already turn people against you so when you reach out for help from family and friends you won't have any support. They will see you as hysterical, crazy, and delusional. The goal of this methodical plan is to intimidate you into silence and isolate you from people because of the abuser's fear of being exposed for who they are behind closed doors.

During this stage, trying to reconcile with him is pointless. He will get great satisfaction as you attempt to mend the relationship. He will be sarcastic, immature, and downright mean. He will twist your words around to make it seem as though you meant something that you didn't mean. Everything you say will be taken out of context and used against you. Your abuser will go on a mission to completely destroy you in every way he possibly can. He will turn your family, friends, children, pastor, and people who don't even know you against you. You will be left feeling mentally and emotionally drained in a state of confusion trying to figure out what is happening.

I know you kept silent because you wanted to protect his reputation. Now the relationship has gotten so far out of control you decide to reach out for help. When you finally confide in someone, no one believes you because you have always talked so positively about him. Besides, he has already damaged your credibility with these people. He has set you up to look like you're crazy, exaggerating, lying, or only out to get him. This can be a very dangerous time because the abuser no longer sees you as having any value. You are worthless to him because he can no longer use you.

You have either stood up for yourself, said "No More!", or he has drained you of all of your resources. As a result, he has no problem murdering you especially if he has already tried to kill you or threatened to kill you. He may even go as far as to tell you to kill yourself. If you are feeling suicidal or having thoughts of suicide please contact the National Suicide Hotline at 1-800-273- TALK (8255). Please contact the National Domestic Violence Hotline at 1-800-799-SAFE (7233) or your local domestic violence women's shelter for assistance with creating a safe exit strategy plan. If you are in immediate danger, please call 911.

Your abuser will delight in your pain as he has moved on. You are left picking up the pieces of the devastation he has left behind. He will flaunt his new relationships in your face or on social media. He will taunt you and try to provoke you to defend yourself, so you can look out of control and crazy to those he has badmouthed. He won't admit any wrongdoing in the relationship. He will play the role of victim. He will convince others to believe that all of the things he has done to you are the things you did to him. It's so important to reach out for help to people who understand and have experienced this type of abuse. Some of the things he's done to you may sound so outrageous that others may have difficulty believing you. Speak up anyway. There are people who completely understand. You're not alone and you matter.

Once you've made up your mind that you are moving on, he may try to reel you back in. If you go back, he will be angry even though he won't show it. He will punish you for standing up for yourself. He will also find it disgusting that you were naive enough to trust him and believe his lies. He feels powerful knowing that he can control you. He may be nice again but this is only the beginning of restarting the cycle of abuse all over again. The most important thing you can do to begin to heal is to not have any contact with your abuser at all.

Triangulation

Triangulation is a form of emotional abuse. The abuser's triangulation goal is to control your emotions and how you react to your abuser's outrageous behavior. Abusers will create situations where they are the center of attention or affection. For example, they will attempt to make you jealous of someone else so they can be the object of desire. They will also create a situation for two people to compete with one another for the abuser's time or attention. This makes him the center of the chaos. This tactic can be used with friends, family members, women he has on the side, or people he doesn't know.

Triangulation was frequently used by my abuser. He used this tactic to keep me away from my family, his family, and friends over the years. He would always tell me that one of his family members said something negative about me. When I would tell him that I needed to call them to clear the air, he would tell me it wasn't my place to confront them. He said it was his job to protect me, and that he would "handle" them. It turns out, the next time I saw them they gave me the cold shoulder and were disdainful. I no longer wanted to go to his family functions because I didn't want to be treated like an outcast. I reached the point where I no longer wanted to resolve the issues with them. When he spoke to them about resolving the issue, it seemed like they hated me even more.

Then he began to use social media to make his women on the side and other people who didn't know me to dislike me. My hindsight then became 20/20. I realized that he probably didn't make any efforts to resolve what I now believe were made up issues. Here I was upset with some of his family members based on something he told me they had said about me. I can imagine he was doing the reverse with them. I sometimes wonder what he told them I said about them. I understand now that this man had so many secrets and skeletons that he couldn't risk having me and his family interacting with one another. I now understand that he didn't want me alone with them because they just might have liked me enough to tell me the truth about some of his dirty little secrets. This is probably why he never wanted me to visit with anyone by myself. He needed to be there to control and monitor the conversation.

Triangulation also damages your self-esteem. It causes jealousy, insecurity, and emotional imbalance. Your abuser will keep you distracted with tactics of flirting with other women and begging him for attention. You will be so preoccupied with trying to win back his love, affection, and attention you won't notice that this is a huge red flag. Remember these things aren't done in a blatant manner. They are done in a very subtle manner that will make you question your sanity.

Flying Monkeys

Flying monkeys are people who are knowingly and unknowingly manipulated by abusers to further abuse their victim in some manner. These people will join in with the abuser to intentionally taunt or humiliate you as a way to show their support for the abuser. Others will unknowingly harass you by thinking they're doing something good by reprimanding you about your abuser. They may also attempt to convince you to go back to your abuser or for you to allow your abuser to come back to you. They have not seen his cruel and violent side. Flying monkeys are under the impression that he is such a good guy that he would never hurt a fly.

Flying Monkeys are also enablers who will attack your credibility to cover up for the narcissistic abuser. They are also being manipulated by the narcissist. They will comply with the narcissist and meet his every demand for fear of what he is capable of doing to them. When the abuser becomes physically abusive and his actions are no longer a secret, the flying monkeys will blame you for the despicable things the abuser does. They won't hold the abuser accountable for his abusive actions and behavior. An abuser who has flying monkeys to enable his bad behavior only gets worse. As a result, he feels more powerful and in more control because no one is telling him that his behavior is wrong, unacceptable, and that he should stop.

Smear Campaign

An abuser uses the smear campaign tactic when he feels the threat of being exposed. The abuser will talk badly about you and defame you to others face-to-face, on social media, or through any form of communication with others. Their goal is to accuse you of being abusive or being the one with a problem. They'll also try to bait you into publicly responding to defend yourself against their lies. An abuser wants you to hysterically try to defend yourself so he can say, "See I told you she's crazy!"

If you have distanced yourself from your abuser he will also use the smear campaign to reel you back into his chaos. He wants you to defend yourself to people who don't matter. He has already built an alliance with them and they will never believe you. My suggestion, don't waste your time on trying to defend yourself from the smear campaign. Focus on getting out, staying out, and rebuilding your self-esteem, self-worth, and self-confidence. Increase your overall level of self-love that you have for yourself.

Psychopath

A psychopath can be defined as some of the following but not limited to:

- Lacking fear
- Violent
- Lacks realistic goals
- Fails to plan for the future
- Lives a parasitic lifestyle
- Arrogant
- Manipulative
- Boastful
- Lacks boundaries
- Controlling
- Charming
- Pathological liar
- Insecure
- Irresponsible
- Fragile ego
- Easily offended

Psychopaths lack emotions such as shame, guilt, and embarrassment. They can't and don't identify with people who express their emotions. In fact, when you express your emotions to or in the presence of a psychopath they will find it disgusting. They may get angry with you or even laugh at you. Their goal is to humiliate you and make you feel worse. Psychopaths feel entitled to whatever you have. If you attempt to create boundaries you become public enemy number one. You might as well have a target on your back or forehead. Psychopaths are bullies who don't like boundaries. They will twist your words or accuse you of doing something they are doing themselves. These types of people are cowards who don't fight fair.

Psychopaths will play psychological games to control you. They will withhold sex, give you the silent treatment by ignoring you, making you think you are not good enough, blame you for everything, and not take responsibility for their actions.

Mama's Boy

When we hear a man describe himself as a mama's boy, his mother describes him as one, or he says that he and his mother are very close, and we think of this as a great thing. The first thought that comes to mind is, "If he is close to his mother he must know how to treat a woman." Wrong! In some situations these mama's boys have built up animosity towards their mother and take their anger out on the women they date or marry. These men lack of respect for women. They call women degrading names. They speak highly of their mother in public, but behind closed doors they express their disdain for their mother. Some men may talk like a baby or 5 year old boy when speaking to their mother face-to-face or on the phone. The moment she is out of his presence he rages with anger because she always wants to know what he is doing. He may share how she's overbearing, treats him like a little boy, doesn't allow him to have his own life, and doesn't allow him to discipline his own children. This type of man will have issues with the need to constantly assert his manhood. Even though he is abusive he expresses his disgust for how his mother allows his father to physically abuse her and accepts other forms of abusive behavior towards her.

The relationship may be so unusually close that the mother puts the son in a position where he feels as though he has to choose between his wife, girlfriend, or children. She may become so overbearing that she has to know his every move. He can't have a life outside of his mother. If he doesn't report in to her she may become ill or suffer some kind of physical injury that requires his immediate attention. She will make him feel guilty for not doing what she wants him to do.

She will have an issue with his relationship and with his wife. She will tell him that he can't trust his wife, and that his wife will never love him the way she does. Even though she tells him that his wife can't be trusted, she will never give him a valid reason or any reason at all. She will cause the son to become paranoid about his relationship with his wife. He won't trust his wife. As a result, he will feel like he can only trust and depend on his mother.

The mother will say or do things to the daughter-in-law and then deny any ill intent. She will also use forms of Gaslighting to attempt to throw the daughter-in-law off balance. She will accuse the daughter-in-law of being sensitive and taking this the wrong way. The things she does are very subtle and include back handed compliments. She will also accuse the daughter-in-law of trying to break up the relationship between her and her son. Meanwhile, she is trying to break up her son's marriage or relationship. If she doesn't get her way or finds it difficult to break up her son's relationship; she will always have some kind of crisis, illness, or emergency that needs her son's immediate attention. She will also try to turn your children against you by going against anything you tell your child to do or not to do. She will reprimand both the son and the daughter-in-law right in front of the children. This tactic is used so that she can diminish their authority with their children. If you notice a change in your child's behavior such as your child not listening to you or being disrespectful after these encounters, you may want to limit their interactions with this woman.

Women have sons. They tell their son to not hit women and respect women. Don't be like your daddy! The sons will do all of the things she wished she would have gotten from her husband or boyfriend. When the son grows up and has a girlfriend or wife; this same woman who told him to treat his wife or girlfriend like a queen, all of a sudden seems jealous of his wife or girlfriend for receiving the love and respect that she deserves from a man.

The next time you hear a man describe himself as a mama's boy, know that he's actually his mother's surrogate husband. In this type of mother-son-relationship, the mother is either single, divorced or the man in her life is emotionally and mentally weak.

If she is married and her husband is around he has been emasculated. She views him as weak or she no longer respects him because he is abusive towards her. She also makes sure that there is tension between the father and son. She makes sure that the father knows that the son takes precedence over him. The father then becomes jealous of the son because of how the mother reveres the son. The mother and son have a relationship that doesn't include her husband. This immense pressure to please his mother causes him to have the inability to have healthy relationships with other women. This is often contributes to a man's behavior of constant cheating and a lack of respect for women. He knows that he can't release his anger and frustrations out on his mother so he takes it out on the multiple women he comes in contact with. As a result, he is not capable of having a healthy relationship or marriage with a woman.

Narcissistic Behavior

I just couldn't understand how he could call me names, degrade me even in front of the police, physically abuse me, and then turn around and act as though he is the poor innocent victim. It pained me that he acted as if nothing had ever happened. I was in jaw-dropping shock when he started talking to family members that he said he hated and had forbidden me to talk to. He would call his mother names and then become a doting son to her face.

He would say he hated his father and then praised him to the public on social media. I never could understand why a particular cousin hated me. At times, we would get along great. As soon as a little time passed, out of the clear blue sky she hated me. I never knew why. I would tell my husband, "Well let me call her and find out why." He would always say, "Fuck her, you don't have to kiss her ass." One time I went against his wishes and I actually did call her.

We had a Christmas family gathering at our home. I noticed his cousin kept rolling her eyes at me. I didn't want to address it during the event, but I made it a point to call her the following evening. I asked his cousin why she was rude to me, and she said she thought I had talked about her to my friend. I explained to her that my friend was going through some personal issues and she was grouchy with everyone including me. My friend's attitude or moodiness had nothing to do with me, her, or anyone else who was there. I also wondered why my friend would come if she knew she was going to be in a bad mood.

I understood that my friend was also very tired from her drive, and also the single mother of a very active toddler. I explained to his cousin that I don't share my past issues that I have had with someone to any of my friends. So my friend's attitude had nothing to with her. My friend knew nothing about me and the cousin's rocky history.

So many times we can move on, but the person we told about a situation may not be able to move on from the issue. My friend had no idea that we had a rocky history. I asked her why she didn't talk to me and ask me what was going on. I felt like a broken record telling her that if she has an issue with me to please talk to me about it.

I won't know you have an issue unless you tell me. I wanted to keep the lines of communication open. Months and years later this proved to be useless. She continued with her rude and inconsiderate behavior. She always found some reason to have an issue with me. Not surprisingly, this is the same cousin who was forced to resign from her job for selling confidential client information out of her job's database.

It wasn't until I saw how he turned on me and lied about me that I realized he was the reason no one liked me. He was the reason I had an unknown issue his cousin. He became best buddies with exes and church members He said he disliked because they were hypocrites, and cousins he had labeled as whores, liars, and troublemakers. I never saw this behavior in them which I kind of brushed off, but he never wanted me to hang out with them.

One time when he was at work I went to visit his mother's brother and his wife. He got so angry and told me I better not go over there again by myself. Well, hindsight is always 20/20 because this was the same aunt that warned me, and told me how they were all liars and would do nothing but use me. Not knowing I was in a brainwash cycle of abuse, I ignored her warnings, and made excuses. I told her my husband was different from the rest of his family, that he had matured, and would never do anything to hurt me.

One of the most painful times was after I left. His cousin and his cousin's wife, who are both teachers who initially laughed about the abuse, finally realized the severity of the abuse. They called to check on me and my daughter. What still resonates with me today is that they both said in a serious tone, "We knew they were using you, everyone knew they were using you but you!" My heart sank. I held back my tears. I asked, "Why didn't anyone say anything?". Their response was, "We thought you knew and liked it. We didn't understand why you would even be with him." This is when I began to understand from his cousin the dark side of who he was as a child growing up and even stories about him as a teenager. They also told me that he changed into a different person once he met me. They couldn't believe the transformation of him going from a rude and non-ambitious to this really nice guy who wanted something out of life.

Once again it was confirmed that he was not focused, driven, ambitious, and intellectually stimulated. His cousin described him as a "thug." His cousin explained to me why he had distanced himself from my abuser, and only started coming back around because he "changed for the good" once we got married. I continued to listen to countless stories his cousin shared even about the parents. Some things surprised me, others didn't. When it came to someone I thought I was going to spend the rest of my life with, and had poured so much of myself into, I was in complete heartbreaking shock.

After he started beating me, choking me, body slamming me, and holding knives to my throat, he began to openly flirt with women whenever we would go out, or show me a picture of a woman he was talking to on social media. He also started flirting with his exes online. He was bold enough to tell me what they would say back to him along with other women. He would always pause to see my reaction, and after he started beating me I learned to not say anything at all because I was afraid he was looking for a reason to go ahead and kill me.

I still struggle with being angry with myself because I didn't leave a long time ago. How in the world could someone get away with treating another person so badly? I think what makes it so bad is that he would always laugh about the mean things he would do or say to me. He would mock me as I would try to explain why what he was doing to me was wrong. And he would mock me as I how I would try to escape him as he choked me.

Over the years he would make insulting comments, or out of nowhere make remarks that insulted people at various functions we would attend. Sometimes his comments would clear a room, other times it left people feeling very awkward, and other times some people would just call him an asshole and shake their heads. Was it embarrassing at times? Yes, but he was my husband. I loved him for who he was, and I accepted him flaws and all. However, he went into surgery one person and came out of surgery another person.

He was always rude, yet he softened the blow by disguising it with jokes or humor and he never held back with cursing in front of the pastor, his parents, or anyone else's parents for that matter. I can recall his best friend and his wife telling me how they asked him not to swear in front of their parents. He told them the same thing he told me, "I swear in front of my parents so I won't watch what I say." Sure enough he would swear even worse in front of our parents as if we never asked him not to. I must say I sometimes admired his carefree attitude but not the fact that it was sometimes very nonchalant and inconsiderate.

I can sincerely say, he went in to surgery this person, but he came out as this person on steroids. His humor was replaced with rage, anger, hatred, and physical violence towards me. He began to tell me how everything I did was wrong, and how I couldn't do anything right. I was stunned because I made sure I cooked healthy food for him, purchased whatever the doctor said he needed for a special diet, I ironed his clothes, packed his breakfast, lunch and dinner depending on the shift he was working.

I made sure his side of the bedroom was cleaned up first. I fixed his plate, made his protein shakes and I even served him breakfast in bed when he was sick. I made sure I paid attention to the ostomy nurse when she trained me on how to change his colostomy bag. I paid close attention to the home care nurses as they walked me step-by-step through how to administer his medication through IV and change his wound dressing before the next time they we were to come back. I tried to make sure I did everything right so that he could see how much I loved him and cared for him. The harder I tried the worse things got.

My mother and I had been estranged for over 7 years because I had finally gotten up the courage to protect myself from years of childhood abuse that drifted in to my adult years. Even though I was estranged from my mother, I still had other family members that I kept in touch with. My abuser distanced me from them. He didn't want me to talk on the phone to them, text them, or allow them to visit me. If I did visit them, I couldn't go without him being present.

He also distanced me from his family. He convinced me that he didn't like them and didn't want to be around them. He also told me he didn't want to be around his family because they didn't like me. I was so confused. I tried to convince him that if his family spent more time around me they would get to know me better. The moment we separated, he formed an alliance with them that caused them to threaten me and speak negatively about me on social media.

One of the biggest warning signs that I missed is while we were apart, when our daughter was an infant, he didn't call to check on her, he didn't pay me child support, and he acted as if she didn't exist. I still get angry with myself because even though he treated me badly during my pregnancy and after our daughter was born; I still married him thinking things would improve. He told me he had matured, he cried hysterically, and even went as far as telling me he had been baptized. He went on and on about how I was the only woman he ever wanted to marry.

After we were married, his oldest daughter's mother filed for child support. This was the second time I had seen him this angry. I was able to calm him down, and get him to see that there was no purpose in following through with the threats he was making towards his oldest daughter's mother. He was so angry that he no longer wanted his daughter to come spend time at our home. He was angry because his daughter chose to live with her mother and visit with us. He wanted her to live with us so he wouldn't have to pay child support and visit her mother.

One day he called me from work and asked who our daughter was laughing with and talking to. I told him I had picked up her sister so they could play. He cursed me out and called me names. He told me I needed to mind my motherfucking business because she was not my child. He said I had no right to have her at our home without his permission. I did as I was instructed and took her back home.

He followed up by telling me and his parents that we weren't allowed to talk to her or have her over to visit. He said she made her choice to be with her mother so let her stay over there. Each time he got his paycheck he would threaten to go do something violent to her mother. He didn't want to pay child support and he was upset that he would work long hours just to get a "short check" as he would call it.

This was a huge red flag that I didn't pay attention to. I didn't know the dynamics of their relationship except for what he had told me over the years. He had convinced me that she was a horrible person and a whore. Based on my experience with him, I now believe that this is not true. I should've known what was coming. He had ignored our daughter when I separated from him before, and then banned his daughter from coming to our home. It was just a matter of time before he would turn his wrath on me. I just never thought that I could or would ever do anything to make him that angry. It turns out, I didn't. When abusers make up in their mind that they need to control you, you don't have to say or do anything to be abused.

If He Lies, He'll Cheat

The truth will always reveal itself. When I first met my abuser I was 18 years old. I hadn't really dated. I was the quiet, naïve, shy, nerd type. I wasn't the girl boys liked in high school or at least they didn't show it. I was in my first year at an all - women's private college when I met my abuser. He swept me off of my feet. He seemed to be interested in the same things as me. He also said he had the same college major. He told me he had to leave school and lost a football scholarship at one college in Virginia because he blew his knee out in football practice. He also said he attended another college on a football scholarship but his knee wasn't strong enough to continue. As a result, he ended up dropping out of school because his football scholarships ended. I later found out that he blew out his knee unloading ice on a truck at an amusement park he was working for during one summer.

After a year of dating, his father enlisted him into the military because he said he wanted him to become a man. He didn't want to go in the military but his father said he had to go since his mother wouldn't allow his father to teach him how to be a man. When he left for the military we continued our relationship, and I even travelled with his parents to his graduation from boot camp. I noticed a change in him. He was obsessed with telling me about a female he met and kept telling me I was the enemy. I thought this was because he was sleep deprived and had been through such a rigorous training. He seemed upset that I didn't get jealous of this other woman. I knew she was married, and he and I were a couple, I thought nothing of it.

Once he got stationed to his location; he started telling me things about more women. The cruel part is that a few of us all had the same name. He laughed about how he would never call us by the wrong name. At this point, I did ask him if he was cheating on me, and he lied and said no. Three years later he admitted to me that he cheated with this other woman with the same name as me. I was crushed. How could someone claim to love me, and do something so vicious and hurtful over and over?

I broke up with him but he kept calling, sending gifts, and poetic letters begging for me to take him back. After a year had passed he casually mentioned that this woman had a baby. I asked him if it was his baby and he said he didn't know. I wanted to know why he didn't know if it was a onetime thing. Then he told me that he asked her and she told him, "No". Over the years he would out of the clear blue say to me, "I wonder if that kid will show up on our doorstep some day?" Once again I am confused. I asked him again, "Is it or is it not your child? Why don't you find out?" I am tired of this sick cat and mouse game that is being played. For years he never confirmed or denied, yet always played mind games with me about it.

After having a child together, years of marriage, and time that I will never get back; I started hearing rumors from some of his family members and friends that he was only using me and had other women on the side. I don't know how many women or children he may have had behind my back during our 20 year relationship and marriage. The only thing I can do is move forward with my life, and only look back long enough to see how far I have come.

He lied about his education, goals, dreams, how many people he had slept with. His mother even lied about her education and other things that I guess they thought would make them look better. His mother bragged about how she would cover for him, and help him cheat on other women (red flag). They both told me those days were over because he had matured. Sometimes we can be so in love with another person and blinded by love that we don't see or heed the red flags and warning signs.

My abuser would verbally and emotionally abuse me in front of his best friend and his wife. The following day when my abuser was not with me they said they noticed how mean he was acting towards me. They warned me and told me that he would never love me the way a husband should love a wife. They explained that he had a highly unusual and inappropriate relationship with his mother. They shared stories from their childhood into adulthood of how my abuser was very jealous, possessive, rude, and a pathological liar.

They emphasized that he would always put his parents before me and that we wouldn't look out for my best interest. I was in complete denial. I didn't believe he would do this. His words would say one thing, but his actions would say another. He would also swear profusely in front of their parents and when asked not to, he would swear even more in front of their parents. In the end, I wish I had listened to them and run like hell.

His aunt, who is an in-law, warned me and told me not to trust anything they say. She said he was brainwashed by his mother and her youngest sister. She also advised me not to leave my daughter alone with them because they will probe her for personal information and turn her against me. I already felt ostracized and was having difficulties with my daughter. I was experiencing the cold shoulder from my daughter, but didn't know exactly why. It didn't surprise me when his aunt told me that in-laws are not considered family. They only considered the siblings and their children and grandchildren family. She said he was a spoiled brat who would never live up to the responsibilities of being a good husband and father.

I immediately defended him, and tried to explain that he said he matured. Although I was offended, I continued to listen. I listened because deep inside I knew what she was saying was true. My abuser's actions never matched up to his words. I was in denial and found this very hard to hear. She explained how he and his family will lie and tell you the sky is green and make you believe it. She even reminded me of some situations that had taken place in the months leading up to our conversation. These things made me think. They also made me fearful. How could I face my own reality of the bad decisions I made marrying a man like this? I questioned how I could be with someone whose behavior wasn't consistent. His aunt accurately described her observations, descriptions, and the magnitude of the dysfunction that I felt trapped in.

I once got into a major argument with my sister because my abuser stole her husband's cassette tape. When my sister told me I didn't believe her. When I asked my abuser, he initially said, "No." Then he laughed and said, "Yup, I hit them up for that Dr. Dre'!" I was in shock. I couldn't believe he would steal something, lie, and then laugh about it. I couldn't believe he would put me in such a compromising position. Since he refused to give me the cassette tape, I purchased a new tape for her husband. These are just a few examples of the many lies he had told during our time together.

When we first started dating I shared my goals, dreams, plans, and vision of what I wanted to achieve in life. I asked him about his plans for his life. I wanted to know his short-term and long-term dreams and goals. I asked because I have always been a very ambitious, focused, and driven person. I have always been motivated. I wanted to share this so that any one I dated could be very clear on what my life focus was. I wanted to be equally yoked with my mate. If we weren't on the same page, we could go our separate ways and not waste each other's time.

He told me he had gone to a university in Virginia and blew his knee out in football. As a result, he transferred as a walk-on to a university football team in Ohio and was cut from the team because of his knee injury. He told me that his major was also in psychology and that he too wanted to have his own business helping people. I couldn't believe it! I was ecstatic. He was someone who shared my interests and didn't view me as a nerd. I was in heaven as I thought I met the person of my dreams. It was unreal how we shared so many of the same interests. He was like a mirror image of me. He would even joke at times and tell me, "Hey, I am the male version of you! We are going to be a power couple Ladybug."

I later accidentally found from his best friend and his wife that none of this was true. I had taken our daughter over to play with their children at their home. We were watching television, and the university in Virginia came on and I said, "Oh, it's a shame my husband hurt his knee and the school let him go without even offering to give him rehab." You could hear a pin drop. A few people left the room, a few others stayed and observed, and his best friend and his wife asked me to repeat myself. They asked me when my husband supposedly played for this team. I told them the details of what I had been told over the years. They said, "Oh wow, he's never left this area. He never went to school there, so there's no way he could have played football there." As for the school in Ohio, he only attended that for less than a year due to bad grades and not showing up for classes."

Throughout the years I could never understand why he lied to me about big and small issues. He enjoyed laughing at my frustration when I asked for the truth. He taunted me with quotes from movies like, "You can't handle the truth!" while he laughed uncontrollably and ignored my tears and cries of hurt and pain. Whenever I knew for a fact he was lying, he made it seem as if I was crazy and that I was, "Making it up in my head".

When I stopped crying about these issues, I started speaking out about how badly he was treated me. When he overheard me confiding in a friend about how hurt I was from years of dealing with the pain of his lies and manipulation, he began to get physical with me. He started to poke me in my face, grab me by my arm, and bump me into the wall. Unfortunately, I still didn't recognize this as physical abuse and I stayed with him.

Although it frightened me, I didn't view it as life threatening. I blamed myself because I thought if I hadn't questioned him he wouldn't have become angry with me. So I apologized to him for questioning his cheating and making him mad. Instead of telling the truth about beating me, he told people that I couldn't handle his sickness, that I fell apart and no longer wanted him.

If He'll Cheat, He'll beat

I'm definitely not saying that a woman should be physically abused in any way. However, my abuser would literally have tears coming out of his eyes when someone would get slapped on TV or in a movie. I didn't understand this type of humor, but I also didn't understand why he was so violent and over the top the first time he beat me. Why not a slap on the face like in the movies? It was like he had a ton of built up anger towards me and everyone else he didn't like. I still wonder to this day why he had so much rage and anger. This is the same question the pastor or shall I say "his pastor" would ask me, "Why is he so angry and childish? I just don't know where all of his anger is coming from." I couldn't answer this for his pastor. I was just as baffled as the pastor.

During my journey I learned that an abuser's heart rate goes down when he attacks you because he's in control and this calms him down. This is not rage as we would assume, this is the abuser's way of beating you back into submission. Some days I felt like he enjoyed seeing how he had stolen something from me after he beat me the first time. Something from the pit of my soul, something inside of me felt like it didn't shine as bright or not at all anymore. He told me he beat me because it made him feel like a man and he didn't want me to leave him. He said he was afraid of losing me. I guess I would have questioned him as to why in the world would you think I would stay, but I figured I would pass on what he would call a provoked beat down.

After we split up this last time, I didn't miss the fear, intimidation, and him constantly reminding me of what he was capable of doing to me. My daughter and I no longer had to barricade ourselves in the master bedroom for fear of him barging in to verbally or physically abuse me. For a while, I thought I missed him. It turns out, I didn't miss him. I missed the person he pretended to be.

CHAPTER 4

Save Yourself

"Your silence won't protect you." ~Audre Lorde

Domestic Violence is a rapidly increasing dangerous and deadly epidemic in the United States. Domestic violence and abuse does not discriminate. I always thought if I did all of the right things it would never happen to me. I was wrong. Domestic violence does not take into consideration your race, income, class, age, ethnicity, religion, level of education, or marital status. If you are a female you are at a high risk of being the victim of domestic violence.

The United States Department of Justice reports approximately 95% of domestic violence victims are women. Every 15 seconds a woman is beaten in the United States. Each day in the United States an average of 4 women are murdered by their spouse or partner. This statistic is staggering. What's even more disturbing, 75% of these deaths occur after the woman has told her abuser she wants to leave, after a woman has attempted to leave her abuser or has left her abuser. I can't stress enough the importance of working with a professional Domestic Violence expert to create a safe exit strategy plan. Don't make the fatal mistake of hinting to your abuser or telling your abuser you want to leave or that you are even thinking about leaving. Leaving an abuser is not a task you want to take on by yourself. Please reach out for assistance from your local women's Domestic Violence shelter or contact the National Domestic Violence Hotline at 1-800-799- SAFE (7233).

Save Yourself

In an instant my life was turned upside down and inside out. I felt like I was in a snow globe, a blender. I was feeling shaken and stirred. I had experienced something I never thought would happen to me. After having a great time the day before and enjoying fireworks -- the following day was filled with an unexpected explosion right inside of my own home. Months prior to this, my abuser had gone through a horrible surgery that not only left him in bad physical shape, but also changed him mentally, emotionally, and spiritually.

No one could have ever told me this person would have changed so drastically in the blink of an eye. Yes, I noticed a change in his personality, but I thought it was just a matter of him getting through the rough recovery process or the effects from taking multiple medications.

The doctors wanted me to have him admitted to a personal care home, and I refused because I wanted him to be in the comfort of his own home. I had a home care nurse come to the house to make sure he would be taken care of properly. He came home with an unexpected PICC line, wound vac, colostomy bag, and other medical complications. The nurses trained me on how to administer his medication through his PICC line, how to change his colostomy bag, and how to care for his wound in the event of an emergency. I just believed he would pull through, and I was willing to do whatever needed to be done for him to survive this terrible ordeal.

His personality had changed so drastically that it got to a point where he told me everything I did was wrong. No matter how hard I tried to make sure he was comfortable, had his medications, colostomy supplies, proper food, and whatever he needed it was never good enough. The harder I tried to please him the worse he continued to treat me. I got desperate one day, and I called his mother to let her know he was sleeping until 2:00PM and 3:00PM each day.

I asked her if she would come visit him or possibly take him out to lunch. When he found out I did this, he was furious because he said he didn't want to be bothered with his mother. When he came home from spending time with his mother, he brought me flowers, cried, and thanked me for taking care of him. Later that evening he got angry because his colostomy bag was leaking. He began to call me names and told me that I better not call his mother again. He explained what was going on under our roof and what he was feeling was no one's business. He told me he didn't want his mother to know he was having bad days because he didn't want her to worry. I thought to myself, to hell with my feelings or well being.

A week prior to my first initial beating, he got angry because I forgot to make his protein shake at a specific time, and he wanted me to look up something for him online. I told him he should be making his own shakes at this point, and he could certainly look up something on his own online. He told me he liked for me to do things for him. After I stood my ground and wouldn't complete either task, he threatened to bust me in my face. It's not that I ignored this BIG red flag; I just didn't think he would ever do something so violent, especially not to me. I thought he was just blowing off some steam because his colostomy bag was very active this particular day.

I was loyal, committed, and even put up with disrespect from some of his family members because of my love for him. I thought because he expressed his anger towards the surgeon, and some other issues he had been having with some of his family members; that he was just blowing off steam and taking it out on me. I didn't think for a split second that he would ever go as far as to act on it. I did notice he was very angry after the surgery. Yes, as women we like to nurture and fix people. I thought if I loved, supported, and reassured him that I was going to be there for him no matter what. We would get through it together and he would find some comfort in that.

Protect Yourself

Protecting yourself, your child, or children is imperative. I struggled for so long as to whether or not I should stay with my husband or leave him. I wanted my daughter to grow up with both of her parents in the same home even if it meant me having to be miserable in a horrible marriage. I was willing to give up my happiness so that my daughter could experience growing up with her mother and father no matter how bad it was getting for me. One of my wake-up calls to finally protect myself was my daughter's health. Our daughter was sweating profusely all of the time, had trouble concentrating, and struggling in school. After the beatings started she became terrified in school thinking her father was going to show up to the school to harm her because she would call the police. She was also afraid to leave me at home by myself with him for fear that he would begin beating me, and she wouldn't be there to call the police. No matter how I tried to ease her fear, she was still afraid that her father would and grandfather would eventually kill me.

It took me a long time to realize that I needed to put myself first. I needed to put myself first by protecting myself. I didn't protect myself because I was struggling with an internal conflict of not wanting him to go to jail for what he was doing to me. Each time the police came to our home I made excuses for him, I covered in the name of love. When our daughter called the police I didn't want him to go to jail because of his colostomy bag. The policeman even told me that they had nurses who would assist him with changing his colostomy bag. I thought he was upset because he had not worked in months, had multiple surgeries, and was just frustrated with his physical condition. I didn't know I was in the vicious cycle of Domestic Violence.

I also didn't want to tell the police what he was doing to me because he would always tell me he was a black male with no police record. I didn't want to tarnish his record or image. I thought it was a onetime incident and this couldn't possibly be my husband. It turns out the first beating was the opening of Pandora's Box. Once he got a taste of beating me and because I didn't report him, he began to enjoy seeing me in fear. The sickest part about whenever he would physically abuse me, he would be wearing a white wife beater.

He started wearing them because the shirt would help keep his colostomy bag positioned in one place. I would literally shake when he would walk towards me. My mouth would become very paste like and dry out. I would visibly shake to the point where I couldn't stand. He would laugh so hard and make jokes about how my knees were knocking so loud the neighbors could hear them. The sad part is that he always bragged about all of the things he had gotten away with over the years. It was at that moment that I began to realize that I had enabled and encouraged his bad behavior over the years by going along to get along. I was no longer willing to be manipulated, and I wanted to get off of this train wreck of abuse.

On one occasion while he was beating me, our daughter came in the room and saw him sitting on top of me (at this time he was 6'1" 400lbs) on the floor choking me and holding a knife to my throat. She said, "Please let me talk to my mom before you kill her?" "Please stop, if you don't stop I am going to call the police." He dared her to call the "motherfuckin'" police. As I was struggling to breathe, I tried to tell her not to call the police. I just thought if I could calm him down things would be better.

Our daughter was brave and called the police anyway; he yelled and screamed at her daring her to call the police as he didn't think she would. He got up from on top of me and leaned down in her face with the knife still in his hand and yelled, "I see who's side you are on you little BITCH! FUCK YOU, you BITCH! If you want your goddamn mama you can have her. I will gut that bitch like a fish. That's how you are going to do me? You called the police on me. FUCK YOU TOO!" My heart ached for our daughter. I thought for sure he would stop once she came in the room. Unfortunately, this became our norm.

I felt alone, ashamed, embarrassed, and I didn't want him to go to jail because I felt like he was all I had. I was reluctant to have him arrested. Once again he had no accountability for his actions. It is very difficult to have someone arrested that you love. I also didn't follow-up and go to the hospital because he bullied me into not going because he said I just want to hurt him by getting an exam.

Even though my neck was swollen, I was bleeding, and my body was sore. I was bruised from being thrown around and I didn't want him to get in trouble with the law. Once again I was trying to prove my love and loyalty to him and I didn't go to the hospital for treatment.

Initially, I was afraid to file for a Civil Protection Order (CPO). Each time the policeman came to our home, they urged me to get the CPO. They told me they couldn't make him leave if I wouldn't speak up because his name was also on the mortgage. I cancelled 3 different appointments with the local Women's Shelter for Domestic Violence before I finally showed up for the 4th appointment. On the 4th appointment I finally showed up to the appointment and followed through with filing for protection.

Prior to filing for the civil protection order, out of fear I fled our home in the middle of the night not knowing WHEN he was going to kill me. The violence was escalating. Everything made him angry. He was always short-tempered and angry about everything. I told him I don't know what to do to make you like me or love me anymore. Why do you always say I do everything wrong? His response as he laughed was, "You even breathe wrong bitch". Like many women of domestic violence, I came home to the scene of the crime.

He sweet talked me with his poetry and smooth words. The honeymoon phase had begun then BAM! The devil that I ran from in the middle of the night showed back up within two weeks of our return. There I was conflicted all over again. This time I got the courage to follow through. Not only did I file for the CPO, but I also took the policeman's advice on the day we went to court for the CPO. I filed a report with the prosecutor's office for criminal domestic violence charges. When you make the decision to leave your abuser, do not tell him. I made this mistake in an effort to be open an honest.

My abuser threw knives at me, and told me we would have to have a knife fight in order for me to leave. I told him I was not going to have a knife fight with him because he just wanted an excuse to kill me. He knew he could beat me. He had already shown me. I already knew this because he was so much bigger than me. I knew this was a trap, so I refused to engage as he threw the knives at me.

If you are experiencing physical abuse, please contact your local domestic violence women's shelter for assistance with creating a safe exit strategy plan. You can also contact the National Domestic Violence Hotline at 1-800-799-SAFE (7233) for assistance.

I always think if only I would have been educated on Domestic Violence. I firmly believe I would have been more decisive in making my decisions. I wouldn't have run without a plan. I would have stayed and done all of the things I learned to do after the fact. I was very blessed to have very supportive policeman. When the policemen found out that I came back to my home, they made special rounds to pass my home to ensure my daughter and I was safe. The local women's shelter was also very supportive. The legal advocates from the local women's domestic violence shelter showed up to court with me for support and helped me with my victim's legal rights. I realized that even though my abuser told me no one else loved me or cared about me, it was not true. There are people who care about you and you are not alone.

So often I would find myself starting my sentences with the following examples below. If you find yourself starting any of your sentences with these words, it is a form of self-abuse. You did the best you knew how at the time. Be kind and gentle to yourself.

- "If only I would have…"
- "I should have…"
- "I could have…"
- "If I had not…"
- "If I didn't…"
- "What if I would have…?"
- "What if I could have…?"
- "What if I did…?"

Remember, you can't control someone else's actions. Quite frankly I never thought I would ever be the victim and a survivor of domestic violence. It is not your fault when someone decides they want to blind side you by physically abusing you. You must always protect yourself first. Report the first and all incidents thereafter to the police, so you can create a paper trail. Go to the hospital so you have your injuries documented by medical professionals. If you need to file a protection order don't hesitate if your life has been threatened, or you have already been physically abused.

Call The Police

As I stated before, my abuser held me to very high standards to the point where I would constantly have to tell him that I am not perfect patty. I make mistakes too. Over the years he would joke and tell me he would choke me, slam me, beat me, bust my mouth out, and take me for everything I have if I ever thought about leaving him. I didn't know that his jokes were very real threats that he would eventually act upon. My life changed the day he got so angry because my business was not making the kind of money that he thought it should be making. He was angry because he thought I wasn't working hard enough to get my business off of the ground. I told him to calm down but he only got worse. I was not able to dedicate the time to my business because I was trying to keep the entire family afloat.

He was so angry and upset that all I wanted to do was just leave and let things cool off. When I tried to leave with our daughter, once again he told me I would have to have a knife fight with him in order to leave, and he began to throw knives at me. He then told me he was going to slash the tires on my car. As I tried to get by him to hurry up and leave, he grabbed me by the throat and threw me from the kitchen to the family room. At this point, I am in complete shock again as he began body slamming me, hitting me with a laundry basket, a tall metal kitchen stool, and broke a tray table over my back. He sat on me as he choked me. I was on the floor in pain semi-conscious and confused.

My head had hit the floor so hard I saw bright silver light. As he beat me, he called me a dumb bitch, silly bitch, and a bad bitch as he kept yelling how he hated his life. He added that I am pathetic and disgusting to look at because I am a constant reminder of people's personal failures. He held the knife to my throat and stomach and told me he would gut me like a fish.

Our daughter yelled out, "Please let me talk to my mom before you kill her?" "I am going to call the police!" He yelled profanities at her and got angry because she called the police. Even though he called her names as he tried to leave the house before the police arrived our daughter was still very brave.

In an instant of the first initial beating, I realized I had become a statistic. I didn't realize like so many women I covered for my abuser. I explained to the police that he had a very bad surgery and had not worked in months. This is not who he is, and he is just stressed out. He had been through a very traumatic medical experience. I didn't want him to go to jail because he had a colostomy bag, and I thought he just made a mistake. The policeman reassured me it was not a mistake.

The policeman asked me why I had blood on my shirt, and why my neck was red with handprints. I made excuses because I didn't want him to get into any legal trouble. As a result of me not telling the policeman what my abuser had done to me, they took him to his parent's apartment. He was not permitted to come back to the house on this occasion for the rest of the weekend.

Go To The Hospital

The policeman asked me if I needed to go to the hospital. Yes, I should have gone to the hospital but I knew it was a trick question. If I would have gone to the hospital I would have been admitting that I had been physically assaulted despite how I looked. The policeman gave me a pamphlet for the local domestic violence women's shelter which went missing once my abuser came back home. For days after this particular incident my neck, back, and head were hurting and swollen very badly. My abuser said it was not a beating because he didn't use a close-handed fist. He did let me know it made him feel powerful and like a man.

I didn't know that once the cycle of physical abuse starts it does not stop. My abuser would tell me stories of how he grew up watching his father beat his mother, and vowed he would never ever do that to me. He would have nightmares and flashbacks of his father beating his mother. I would comfort him and thought I could fix the pain of his past not knowing that boys who witness domestic violence are twice as likely to abuse their own wife or girlfriend and children when they become adults.

I can't stress enough the importance of calling the police, filing a police report, and going to the hospital. When we got to court he and his attorney said the physical abuse never happened. Since I didn't have previous police reports or medical records of abuse, he lied and said the abuse never happened. My legal advocate from the local women's shelter would come to criminal court for support, and she shared with me that she had been physically abused for 19 years. She finally had enough and called the police, and when they went to court the judge wouldn't listen to any other accounts of physical abuse except for the times the police came to their home.

File For An Order Of Protection

I was instructed by the policeman to file an order of protection. In some states they are also referred to as Protection From Abuse (PFA) or generally known as a Restraining Order. The policeman told me they couldn't keep coming to the house because my abuser had a right to be there. He also told me I needed to get the order of protection before they had to come get me and take me out of my home in a body bag.

This was during one incident when it took 5-6 police officers to keep my abuser off of me. Like many people I didn't want to file for an order of protection because I saw it as a death sentence. I didn't want to make my abuser angrier, and I didn't want him to get into legal trouble.

Months had gone by before I had finally filed for the order of protection. I had called the women's shelter more times than I can count trying to figure out how I could get him to stop being physically violent towards me. I had even scheduled 3 different appointments to meet with a legal advocate at the women's shelter, so she could walk me through the process of filling out the paperwork and getting the documents filed with the court system.

I cried and I was shaking because I didn't want to do it, but I knew I had to. It was even harder because at the very moment I was headed to the shelter, my abuser sent me messages not apologizing but telling me how much he needed me. He said how I didn't deserve how he was treating me. He continued texting that he was taking his frustrations out on the wrong person. He was so good with his words.

I believed him every time he said he was sorry, bought me flowers, or wrote me eloquently worded poems of apologies that were just for me. But this time I had enough! I no longer wanted to be called a stupid, dumb, ugly, bearded bitch, and any other painful names or degrading description that came to his mind. Just because he was angry at someone else or something I did that he didn't like.

Protect Your Children

Oftentimes women who are abused stay in bad relationships for various reasons. One of the reasons I stayed is because I wanted my daughter to be raised with both parents. I wanted her to grow up in a complete family unit. Once again I was trying to defy any negative statistics. Our daughter still experiences guilt because she couldn't physically help me. At the time of the incidents she was recovering from having a surgical spinal fusion. She was also afraid to come close because she feared being paralyzed if he beat her like he was beating me.

No child should have to witness her mother being physically abused by anyone. This has resulted in nightmares, panic attacks, nervousness, and a drop in academic performance. She was afraid of him because not only did he control and abuse me but he began to taunt her, call her bitch, and insinuate that she was a whore.

He would also drop the remote control on the floor by his foot, call her from upstairs in her bedroom, tell her to come downstairs to the family room to pick up the remote control, and hand it to him. As things began to escalate, she became more of a target of his verbal abuse. He was angry that she called the police and accused her of taking sides.

Prior to the physical abuse he would verbally abuse me and play mind games. He would make degrading jokes about me, and get mad at our daughter for not laughing. She began to snub me and be rude to me in order to please him. As a result, our relationship had become strained. Our daughter thought he walked on water because I never told anyone about the cruel things he had done to me in the past.

Once she witnessed him physically abusing me she was done with him. She no longer viewed him the same, and she was terrified of him. I was the one trying to keep the family together and making excuses for him. I didn't realize how brainwashed I had become. This young child was telling me to leave while I was trying to figure out how to make things work and make it better.

My daughter suffered tremendously during this time. My heart ached for her. One week I received phone calls 3 days in a row from different teachers calling me to tell me that my daughter was struggling in some of her classes. I called the guidance counselor and the assistant principal to schedule a conference call.

I was so embarrassed and ashamed to have to tell them why my daughter was having problems. I explained to them that I was forced to file for a protection order to protect us from my husband and that we had just come back in town from fleeing in the middle of the night from abuse. They were both very supportive, and let me know they would do whatever they needed to do to keep my daughter safe while she was in school. I was in shock when the school administrators told me they often deal with domestic violence and this was a very common occurrence.

They went on to explain that other mothers of children in the school were being abused by their husband or boyfriend. At the time, I was not familiar with the statistics on domestic abuse and violence. The statistics are staggering. Why, why, why aren't there more people having OPEN conversations about not just domestic violence, but getting into the weeds of the red flags, warning signs, how to prevent domestic abuse, and knowing how and when to walk away. My sisters, this is why I made a non-negotiable decision to write this book, get on television, and spread my message and start the Speak Up & Get Out Movement!

All children who witness domestic violence don't experience any or all of these traumatic effects. However, there are a significant number of children who do experience mental, emotional, and physical stress as a result of trying to cope with the traumatic devastation of Domestic Violence. Warnings signs in children affected by Domestic Violence include but are not limited to the following:

- Trouble falling asleep
- Difficulty staying asleep
- Waking up with nightmares
- Unable to focus and concentrate
- Daydreaming
- Panic Attacks
- Anxiety
- Fears for their safety
- Fears for your safety
- Chronic sweating
- Change in eating habits; increased appetite or loss of appetite
- Change in behavior (getting into trouble, alcohol, drugs, hanging with the wrong crowd)
- Decline in performance in school (poor grades)
- Depression
- Post Traumatic Stress Disorder (PTSD)

If your child is experiencing any of these behaviors or symptoms please contact the National Domestic Violence Hotline at 1-800-799-SAFE (7233) or contact your local women's Domestic Violence Shelter. If you don't have this information, the National Domestic Violence Hotline can provide you with the contact information for your local women's shelter. They will be able to give you the information to contact a professional counselor or doctor who specializes in working with children of Domestic

Violence. Don't be afraid to call. I would call sometimes 6 or more times in one day. They have compassion and empathize with your situation and there is no judgment if you just need to talk.

Document, Document, Document

If you know your abuser lies on you, lies to you, or lies to make you look crazy make sure you document everything. Write down the time and place an incident occurred, and save your text messages in your phone if your abuser sends you threatening text messages or if he admits to abusing you. Take screenshots of any social media posts that are directed towards you and print these out. Also forward them to your attorney, prosecutor, or local police department so it is legally on file and documented.

Lock the text messages in your phone, print them, and also forward them to your email address or an email address that your abuser does not have access to. Go to the hospital immediately and get an examination. Be sure to tell the hospital staff exactly what happened to you. Save any emails of your abuser talking about physically abusing you or apologizing for what he has done to you. The apology is not real anyway. It's just a way to reel you back in if the abuser feels like he is losing power and control over you.

Check your state laws to make sure you are legally permitted to record telephone conversations between you, and your abuser without the abuser's consent. This will help you prove physical, emotional, verbal, and mental abuse based on the content of the conversation. Keep your recordings in a safe place. Make copies for yourself and also for the police, attorney, and prosecutor. These recordings may be admissible in court based on your state laws.

After I had finally got up the courage to file for the protection order, I went to the local women's shelter to meet with the legal advocate to prepare for the case. I explained to her that I was nervous about the upcoming pre-trial because during the arraignment, he lied and denied physically assaulting me. I had covered for him so many times when the police would come to our home, and here I was trying to prove in the restraining order report what he had done to me with no hospital records to back me up.

I told the legal advocate about the mean nasty text messages and voicemails he sent me and how he left an email admitting that he beat me. To my surprise she wanted me to print out the text messages and copy the voicemails so they can be used as evidence in court. Here I was just casually mentioning how he admitted physically abusing me in some text messages and voicemails and it turns out they were useful.

I know we are not supposed to have regrets in life but I still wish on this day that I would have gone to the hospital. At the time, I cared more about him NOT going to jail than I did about the well-being of my own life and my overall safety.

I began to record our telephone conversations because I got tired of his accusations. At the time I didn't know it was called Gaslighting. I grew very weary of feeling like I was completely losing my mind. I thought my memory was fading. All I knew is that he would always confuse me, play word salad, accuse me of saying I said something I didn't say, or accuse me of not saying something I know I said.

A few times after he beat me, I would tell him to either go to his parent's home or go to a hotel. After being at the hotel or his parent's house for a day or two he would call me. He was so convincing on these calls that he would make me question myself because he would say I said something that I knew I had not said. I would be so confused to the point that I thought I was losing my memory. I thought maybe I was blacking out. During some of those calls he admitted to choking me, slamming me, hitting me with a stool, laundry basket, breaking a tray table over my back, and holding a knife to my throat and stomach and throwing knives at me on different occasions.

He would always tell me that he never used a closed fist so therefore it was not a beating. He would tell me that he was broken into pieces and he needed me to put him back together. I told him I could no longer try to fix him. I needed to fix me. I needed to understand how I got to where I was. He told me that he loved me and I told him there was no way he could possibly love me based on how he treated. He got angry and said, "If I didn't love you, the police would still be scraping you up off of the floor." This response shook me to my core.

I was so out of it during this time that I didn't even think of these recordings because they weren't voicemails. I finally remembered when I started clearing out files on my computer. I was also glad I found them because he and his attorney kept trying to make it seem as if the abuse never happened and that I was lying. I was hurt and frustrated. I checked my state laws, and luckily it was legal for me to record a telephone conversation with him without his consent. I didn't want to do it, but at this point, I had to save myself. I took a copy of the recording to the prosecutor's office and to the police station. The Prosecutor admitted the recording as evidence, and his own confession on the recording is what allowed him to be convicted of Criminal Domestic Violence; along with probation, no access to a firearm, a fine, jail time if he violated the protection order, and anger management classes.

Check your state and local laws to find out if it is legal to record a phone conversation where you live. Most abusers because they are driven by power and control, they will call you and threaten you or try to sweet talk you to come back. It is very important to document every incident. The key factor is to protect you.

In the end the only person an abuser cares about protecting is themselves because they don't want to go to jail. You can also get a notary to sign the transcription of the voicemails and printouts of text messages, and they may be accepted as evidence in court depending on your state and local laws. Saving evidence is very powerful.

Take screenshots of text messages, or social media posts that are deemed threatening or a part of a smear campaign to assassinate your character. Keep any evidence or documents that can prove your abuser has been violent. Make sure you keep copies just in case your abuser has access to your phone or computer.

My abuser took my phone and deleted his email that he sent to me admitting his abuse towards me. Luckily I had already forwarded the email to the local police station and I also sent it to an email address that he didn't have access to for emergencies. Create a secret email that your abuser knows nothing about, and email the evidence to yourself. This way, if your phone is destroyed the files are backed up.

CHAPTER 5

Prepare, Plan, and Protect

"Woman must not depend upon the protection of man, but must be taught to protect herself." ~Susan B. Anthony

---

Prepare

In the second step of my SPEAK formula I urge you to Prepare. P is for preparing a safety plan, having a Plan B, being financially prepared for unforeseen circumstances, estate planning, knowing your state's marital laws, and having a prenuptial agreement regardless of your assets and income.

The Importance of Having a Plan

For years I didn't tell my friends that my husband would call me names, cheat on me, and lie to me. They had all labeled him as an asshole because he would also call them names disguised as jokes or offensive jokes directed towards them. When I finally got up the courage to tell my 2 friends about the abuse I was surprised and shocked at the responses I received in return.

Instead of getting the support I expected I was met with judgment and condemnation. One friend had experienced domestic violence, and the other said she had not. However, I am amazed at how some women who have never been abused by a man in any kind of way seem to have no clue about what an abused woman has to endure to survive an abusive relationship. Some women can be very judgmental and victim blame.

My friend, who lives several states away, called me one morning to say hello. After a brief greeting she began to tell me how if she was me she would sell her house really fast, leave the state, and get out of the area. She has never been married, and she doesn't have children to take into consideration for planning her life. At the time, I was in the beginning stages of my divorce. I had been pouring money into paying my attorney, and I had to catch up on all of our bills including the mortgage.

When my daughter and I fled during the middle of the night, we left for 2 months and my husband didn't bother paying any of the bills. You may be thinking how he could pay the bills if he was not working. After he kept throwing me and body slamming me. I made it clear to him that if he could lift me and throw me around then he could certainly take his ass back to work, and lift the 60 pound plates on his job that he claimed were too heavy for him to lift.

I tried to explain to my friend that financially I couldn't afford to move. We lived in a good school district for our daughter, and the job market was not welcoming anyone with open arms. She couldn't understand how rough it was for me to be homeless for 2 months. I had already learned my lesson about leaving and not having a plan. I packed up and left in the middle of the night out of fear. She wouldn't listen when I explained that I needed to stay in my home long enough to regroup. After I returned home again to my husband, I made up my mind that never again would I make knee jerk fear filled decisions like I did when I ran with no plan. I was frustrated. I had no support from family or friends. No one wanted to get involved. I had family members who said, "Oh yeah, I talked to your mother and I asked her about you." That is always code for, "Yes, she told me a bunch of things about you and I just want to call you directly and find out if it's true."

There were family, so called friends, church members, and even my high school teacher called to "check on me." I learned the hard way that once they got my business they never called back. Each one of them said, "I will be calling to check on you. I wish I would have known you were going through this. I will come to visit you." The list goes on with empty promises. These people didn't support me in any kind of way.

Some even went as far as to send me requests on social media to gain access to my page to see if I would post my personal business. I learned that these people are not my friends, and family is not always about who you are biologically related to. I didn't ask anyone for money. All I wanted was for someone to show they genuinely cared, and to be accounted for just in case I went missing. I just needed a kind and compassionate friend.

I even called a woman pastor to ask for prayer and have a role model who could share scriptures and wisdom. Her response was, "I won't nurture you and you need to stop crying, and take care of your business." When everyone turned their back on me, I knew I had to figure things out on my own. I knew that I had to turn to God to be my kind and compassionate friend. This forced me to strengthen my trust and faith in God because everyone else had left me and forsaken me. I am actually grateful for each one of these people because they showed me their true colors.

Now that I know their true colors, there is no need for me to try to repaint them or pursue any kind of relationship with them. My situation didn't begin to change until I reached out to the National Domestic Violence Hotline and the local women's shelter for domestic violence for help. The people who showed that they cared for me during my lowest and darkest times weren't friends, church people, or family, but strangers who didn't know me.

I definitely learned the hard way about not having a safe exit strategy plan. I was tired and exhausted at the time when I abruptly left our home. My daughter and I weren't sleeping at night because he would stay up all night long cussing about how he wanted to "Fuck up his surgeon!" And having to smell his colostomy bag all of the time. We had to barricade the bedroom door, so he wouldn't come in and take his frustrations out on me.

When I left, I didn't think about the consequences of leaving everything behind that I had worked so hard for over the years. I didn't even think about my job. The only thing I could think of was how he would joke about choking me, slamming me, beating my mouth out, and killing me. He had already shown me that he could choke me, slam me, and almost killed me.

At times while he was doing those things he would threaten to beat my mouth out and kill me. I know he wanted to beat my mouth out because he hated when people would compliment me on my smile. I didn't want to stick around and let him finish me off. He had almost killed me, and it sent me into an emotional downward fearful spiral.

I can tell you from experience, running without a plan made me feel like a failure at times. Enduring his abuse made me feel like I was unstable and weak. The year before he started beating me, his father threatened to put lead in my head because I told him we could no longer give them money. Rumors were swarming that he had begun to use drugs again and we needed to focus on our priorities.

At the time, I didn't feel safe in my own home. At this point I should have called the police and filed a report against his father. No one should ever take a threat on their life lightly. After my abuser began to physically beat me and tried to kill me, I did report to the police, prosecutor, and judge about the threat his father made against my life. Even though he couldn't be charged with a crime, I still wanted the authorities to know. If I ever went missing or turned up dead, they would know who to begin with.

I look back and I should have gone to the local women's shelter. I just kept thinking in my mind that if I ran I could be far away from him. I thought the further away I was from him the safer I would be. When we came back home he was no longer living in the home.

Each night he would drive by our home and sit outside of the house in his SUV, or he would sit in the driveway at just sit there watching the house. He would sometimes call to tell me that I should put the lights on outside because my husband is a French fry short of a happy meal and it may not be safe to be in such a big house in the dark. He also said he wanted to make sure that I wasn't going to leave again.

Safety Plan & Plan B

Having a safety plan is a vital part of being able to survive while living with an abuser. I didn't have a safety plan because I never thought it could happen to me. I thought I was doing everything right. I thought my abuser loved me enough to not physically harm me. Domestic violence does not discriminate. It does not matter your race, age, religion, educational level, or your socioeconomic status.

Domestic violence can turn you in to an emotional mess – having you stuck not knowing what to feel or why it happened. It is very important to prepare for war in time of peace. I didn't have a safety plan or a plan b. I trusted the words of my abuser even though I shouldn't have. It left me in a state of confusion and in a fight for survival for the well-being of me and my daughter.

I strongly suggest having a safety plan. I didn't have a safety plan and in a moment of fear, panic, and desperation I fled in the middle of the night with my daughter to escape the physical abuse. My abuser repeatedly joked about how he would choke me, slam me, beat my mouth out, and kill me if I ever tried to leave him. He had already shown me he was capable of choking me and slamming me so at this point I knew he meant what he said. I was terrified at the thought of being killed. My entire life had flashed before me too many times. I had never experienced my body shaking the way it began shaking after I had started getting beat. My mouth would dry out and I would get so nervous I couldn't think straight. I had been isolated from my friends and family, and I later realized that he had talked badly about me to his family. I had no one I could turn to for help. I was also living is his small town with no family or friends. This was a big mistake to move somewhere I didn't have my own support system.

Initially, I was afraid to reach out to the local domestic violence women's shelter. At the time I didn't understand how much they could help me. All I wanted to do was run away and escape it all. I look back now, and I think a lot of it was shame and embarrassment. It was also the feeling of who would believe me.

This man was so nice, funny, poetic and charming in public. It also didn't help that I would pretend as though he was the perfect mate when we were in public. I also made excuses for his outrageous immature behavior when we were in public. I asked myself over and over why did I lower my standards, and why and how did I allow myself to get into such a toxic relationship. When I fled in the middle of the night, I didn't know where I was going, or where my daughter and I would live. I just knew we needed to get somewhere away from the violence and abuse.

As I stated before, I want to share my mistakes with you. I want to share information with you that I learned through my experience, and things I wish someone would have shared with me. These are things I wish I would have known. The following are some life-saving techniques and strategies to help you safely transition and get out of a violent abusive situation. Planning an escape is essential. Leaving an abuser is the most dangerous time for a woman and her children. Contact the National Domestic Violence Hotline at 1-800-799-SAFE (7233) or visit www.NCADV.org.

I can't stress enough the importance of contacting the National Domestic Violence Hotline or your local women's shelter. You may have friends and family who have your best interest at heart and have good intentions, but they are not professionals. Their advice could possibly cost you your life. You also want to be careful who you confide in. I confided in my husband's pastor and his wife.

I say his pastor because I moved to my husband's city where I had no family, friends, or church family even though I attended this church as a member. One day after my husband beat me the pastor and his wife came to our home. The pastor left to go meet my husband at his parent's house to counsel with him while his wife stayed with me.

The pastor's wife initially said that I shouldn't stay with someone who was beating me but the pastor said my husband and I should stay together because we had potential as a couple. It was clear that when the pastor returned from speaking with my husband and came to talk to me, he and his wife were clearly not on the same page.

I called his wife again for prayer and words of encouragement because my husband wouldn't stop beating me, and she told me to just go to a church where they praise Jesus and that she needed to go because she had a conference call.

I also called the pastor one day, and had him on speaker phone to try and get him to convince my husband to calm down. It didn't matter because my husband continued to call me bitches and other degrading names while the pastor was on the speakerphone. He even told the pastor he wished I wouldn't have involved the pastor. I told both the pastor and him that's only because my husband wanted to continue to freely beat me without anyone knowing. My husband never wanted accountability.

After my voice was not being heard by the pastor and his wife; I wanted someone to know what was happening because I was afraid of being killed. After my husband's surgery the pastor would come to our home once a week to visit with him.

During one of these visits my husband told the pastor that he has told me several times how he could cut my head off and put it so far back in the woods that no one would be able to find it. The pastor laughed, but somewhere deep down inside I felt like my abuser meant what he said.

This post-surgery husband that surfaced had a certain level of evil that began to manifest in a very scary way. Approximately 2 weeks prior to the first initial beating. I asked him why it seemed as though he hated me. He would roll his eye or suck his teeth at everything I said even though he always claimed to not know how to roll his eyes.

He had become very irritable and demanding. Post-surgery his attitude became, I better do what he said to do when he said do it or else be punished. I asked him if he noticed how mean he was to me, and why did he seem to have such a deep hatred for me. He replied, "I know, I noticed I just can't stand yo' ass." I asked why, and he said, "Well for starters, you are disgusting and pathetic to look at because you are a constant reminder of people's personal failures. I hate you because everything you start you finish. You have the world by the balls. You just sailed through your doctoral program, and I want my PhD too!"

He continued to say that he envied me because it seemed as though I got everything I always wanted out of life. He hated my focus and dedication. I told him that he knew I didn't sail through my doctoral program, and reminded him of all of the times I sat at the kitchen counter crying to him because my doctoral program was so hard.

I asked him how many times I stayed up late at night reading and emailing my professors trying to understand what I needed to do in order to finish. He just yelled, "I call bullshit!". "You got the world by the balls. I am jealous of you, and I resent the fact that you do whatever you put your mind to. I do envy you Tamika, look at my life, I hate this fucking shit bag!"

All of this time that has gone by, and I never knew he secretly hated me. He went on to explain why he hated me. He said, "I am 42 years old and I almost died, and I don't have shit to show for it. I smell like shit all of the time from this fucking bag. I can't go to school because of this fucking bag, and this damn surgeon has fucked me up so bad. I don't even have a damn belly button Tamika. I can't even shit out of my ass. I fart loud as hell out of my stomach and this shit is embarrassing."

I tried to draw attention to the things that he did have like surviving those surgeries, having life to see another day, our daughter, the dog, his parents, food, clothing, shelter, his job, and a supportive wife who was able to keep everything afloat while he recovered. I tried to get him to see that throughout it all we were still blessed.

It turns out that even though we were blessed, we may have been financially stable, but we were emotionally, physically, and spiritually bankrupt. He began to shout that he barely had a job because he hadn't worked in over 6 months. He no longer had the military. He said, "FUCK, if it wasn't for you I wouldn't live in a house like this or drive the cars that I do. I ain't shit! I don't have shit. I wouldn't be able to do this shit on my own." He just couldn't understand that it was a team effort. It was not a mine or his, but ours.

He was angry because the surgeon kept falsifying his medical records and documents so my husband was not able to get paid for several months. I told him to be thankful that even though he wasn't getting paid we were still able to have our basic human needs met.

I finally decided to just listen because the more I tried to get him to see the positive things in life the agitated and angrier he got with me. It was very painful to see someone go from being a calm, cool, and collected person to a very non-stop agitated post-surgery person. Once again, I went in to my nurturing, loving, I can "fix" him and make him all better modes.

My heart ached for him, and I wanted so desperately to help him. I reached out to his cousin and his wife who are both school teachers. I assumed since they were educators that they would understand and have empathy for our situation. I explained how he would choke me, body slam me, and loved holding knives to my throat, and throwing knives at me. I also asked them not to make fun of his colostomy bag the next time we saw them because once we would get home he would take his frustrations out on me and our daughter.

Instead of receiving understanding, compassion, and empathy they began to laugh and mock us. They started grabbing each other by the throat as if it was a joke. His cousin's wife started hitting his cousin on his legs and she said, "See, I can beat him and he won't do anything." His cousin's response was, "See, I can choke the shit out of her and she won't do anything." I was crushed, humiliated, and embarrassed because it is not an easy thing to tell someone you are being abused.

This is especially difficult after you have covered for your abuser for so many years pretending as if you have the perfect marriage and relationship when in reality you are living in a nightmare. Confiding in the wrong people can be very dangerous. When my husband found out that I told them what was happening, I caught hell for it. So my advice to you is to be very careful who you confide in, and always seek professional help.

❖ Think of ways you can protect yourself, and decrease your chances of being harmed. For example, in my case I learned to stay away from the kitchen because knives were my abuser's weapon of choice. I learned to run from him in the house. I wouldn't allow him to get close to my face and yell after he began grabbing me by my throat. I kept my car key in my pocket with my cell phone. I would immediately get close to the front door just in case I needed to grab my daughter and run out of the house.

- If you have a child or children, tell them what they can do in case of an emergency. Teach them how to call 911, escape to a neighbor's home for safety, or run to a local community center for help. If you have the opportunity, do safety drills with your children when your abuser is not around.

- Drink plenty of water. This will keep your brain lubricated and help you to think on your feet. If you don't have a cell phone, try to memorize important numbers you may need in an emergency situation. These numbers can be to the local domestic violence women's shelter, a trusted family member, a trusted friend, and of course 911.

- Map out how you will escape your home. If you live in a house, know what door you will use, or what first floor window you can climb out of. If you live in an apartment building, familiarize yourself with all of the exits for a smoother escape. Have a plan to know where you will go once you escape.

- Have a code word that you can use if there is an emergency, or you are in immediate danger. Share this code word with a trusted friend or family member. Call or text them the word to alert them to call the police for you if you can't do it yourself.

We all face some kind of adversity in life that can be inevitable. It's how we handle these adversities that reveal who we truly are. Have you ever paid attention to the way you respond to critical situations that arise in your life? Like many people, you may not notice the small things like how many times a day you complain about what's going on in your life, or how often you say something negative about your situation.

How do you respond to unexpected situations in your life?

> I blame myself - why does this happen to me?
> I get upset and tense. I feel overwhelmed with emotion.

Are you a reactive or proactive person when it comes to handling issues that arise in your life?

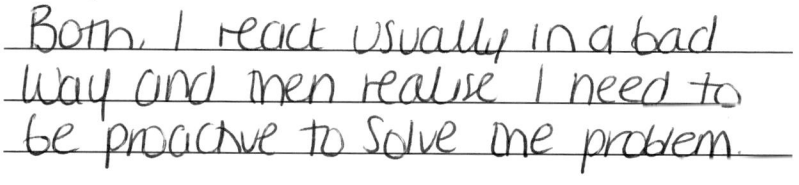

> Both. I react usually in a bad way and then realise I need to be proactive to solve the problem.

Do you ignore red flags or do you take action and prepare in advance to deal with a situation that could possibly arise?

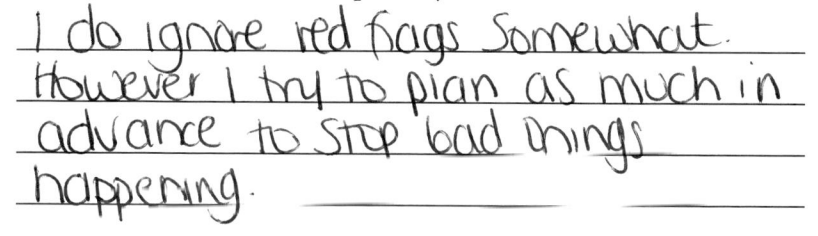

> I do ignore red flags somewhat. However I try to plan as much in advance to stop bad things happening.

In an ideal situation, we would all want to be proactive. However, we know that when we experience abuse making important decisions can be hard to do. Depending on the situation you could be a reactive or proactive person. Being prepared with a safety plan and plan b plays a significant role in how you react to a situation.

Not having a safety plan or a plan b can cause you to be reactive to an event that has occurred. As a result, these knee-jerk decisions can further complicate the situation. You will spend more time and energy trying to "clean up" the mess of the reactive decision. In my situation, I made a reactive decision to flee in the middle of the night with no plan or support.

I also didn't pray about my situation to the extent that I should have. Making proactive decisions are much healthier than reactive decisions. A proactive plan lowers stress, provides clarity, and gives you the courage to know if you need to execute the plan you can do so with confidence.

Benefits of Having a Plan

The first benefit of having a plan b is that you will be very clear and calm in your emotions. When your emotions are not under control, it is very difficult to function when you have been thrust into the middle of a crisis. It is also hard to trust that God will carry you through your situation. You need to remain calm, focused, and keep a positive attitude. This is what I call having that fearless unshakeable faith that you will be okay.

Having a plan b is not anticipating that something will happen. However, when there are red flags, having a plan b is imperative. Being prepared helps you to see a situation for exactly what it is. It allows you to make rational decisions that will in turn protect you and not your abuser. Your abuser showed you how much he cared about you when he began abusing you. This plan will secure a better future for yourself and your children. You have a better chance of having the best possible outcome.

Seek assistance from professionals who can help you prepare a safety plan. Don't be afraid to contact your local women's domestic violence shelter. If you don't have their information, contact the National Domestic Violence Hotline 1-800-799-SAFE (7233), and they can provide you with resources in your local area. As you seek assistance from your local domestic violence women's shelter, write down your plan of action. Think about some of the following things:

What jobs skills do you have?

_____

_____

_____

_____

❖ Speak Up & Get Out! ❖

Do you have any gifts, talents, or hobbies that can generate an income for you?

_____
_____
_____
_____

What are you good at doing that comes easy to you? Can you make money legally from doing it?

_____
_____
_____
_____

How much money will you need to meet your monthly expenses? (rent, groceries, utilities, personal items, clothing, medication, etc…)

_____
_____
_____
_____

What will you do to find a job? (Attend a job fair, employment office, networking, or draft/update your resume')

_____
_____
_____
_____

As I have previously stressed, don't share your plans of leaving with anyone. Especially not with your abuser if you know for sure he is violent. Get out of the passenger's seat of your life and get into the driver's seat. You are now in control of your life. I believe there is a divine calling on each of our lives. Our God, Higher Power, Source, Buddha, Allah has created doors just for us to walk through.

Being proactive in your everyday life will affirm you are living with intention and direction. Each decision you make with an intended purpose and outcome will be the key to your survival. I challenge you to take the time to really examine how you respond to situations that occur in your daily life.

When you do, you can determine what changes need to be made in how you handle stressful situations that arise in your life. Once you identify your strengths and weaknesses, you can begin to improve how you get through a tough and difficult situation.

Take a moment to write down your strengths and weakness. Once you have identified your strengths, start affirming those strengths in yourself.

_____
_____
_____
_____
_____
_____
_____
_____
_____
_____
_____
_____
_____

CHAPTER 6

Enforce Boundaries

"We change our behavior when the pain of staying the same becomes greater than the pain of changing. Consequences give us the pain hat motivates us to change." ~Henry Cloud

---

Enforce Boundaries

The third step in the SPEAK formula is to Enforce Boundaries you have created in your life. It is very common for toxic controlling abusive people to have a sense of entitlement which leads to a lack of having personal boundaries. The lack of having personal boundaries is also a sign that they have a lack of respect for you as a person and human being.

The level of self-respect you have for yourself, and having healthy self-esteem will enable you to create boundaries and more importantly enforce those boundaries. If your self-image of how you view yourself is distorted, you will lack self-respect and suffer with self-esteem related issues. You are putting yourself at risk to attract toxic, abusive, and controlling people into your life. Lacking a healthy level of boundaries can quickly turn you into a people pleaser.

Having boundaries for your life is very healthy. Creating strong boundaries and enforcing those boundaries bring clarity to our lives. This clarity allows us to have a better understanding of who we are as well as how we relate to others. Establishing boundaries for yourself will empower you to decide how you will be treated by other people. The boundaries you set for yourself allows other people to be aware of what you will or won't allow them to say or do to you.

You establish boundaries to state what behaviors you will or won't accept. We can learn how to set boundaries based on our instincts, and how someone makes us feel. The boundaries you set can be for the protection of your physical, emotional, sexual, financial, spiritual, and mental health. You and only you can determine the limits of what is comfortable or uncomfortable for the way someone makes you feel. A healthy solid set of boundaries will give you the comfort of knowing you are protecting yourself from toxic, ignorant, hateful, and mean people who have no empathy and lack remorse.

If you are accepting lying, cheating, abuse, manipulation, or any abusive behaviors, you don't have a firm set of boundaries established in your life. As a result, you are in a sense letting people know you will accept anything from them just to be a part of their life. It's a mentality of, "Having a piece of a man is better than not having a man at all." You are sending a strong message that says, "I don't value who I am." And when you don't value who you are it makes it very difficult to create and enforce boundaries.

This also creates a huge challenge for having the courage to walk away from what no longer serves you in a positive manner. When you accept these bad behaviors, you are telling your abuser or even abusers that you will accept their bad behaviors under their conditions. This sends a message to your abuser that your needs, self-worth, self- respect, and self-esteem are not a priority. You then feel frustrated because you feel like a doormat, but you have extended a detrimental invitation for your wants and needs to be a low priority or no priority at all.

When it comes to having boundaries, you have to look at people as if they fall into two different groups. These two groups consist of the weeds and seeds in your life. Think of your boundaries as a garden, this is your life. You will have to keep your garden free of unwanted weeds. These weeds will overtake your life. The weeds in your life will wear you down leaving you drained. Rid your life of the weeds, and replace them with seeds that will grow, multiply, and beautify your life.

I never thought I would become a victim of domestic violence. I would have argued anyone down if they would have told me my abuser was capable of physically abusing me. I was so brainwashed by my abuser, and hung onto every word he said that I no longer made decisions independent of him. I no longer valued who I was. I went from a confident woman to realizing one day I had allowed someone to completely destroy my self-worth, self-esteem, and even compromised my morals and values.

On my journey I now realize that I worshipped the ground he walked on. I always put him first. I always made sure he had what he needed and wanted for that matter. I made sure when it was time to eat I fixed his plate first and he got the, "Big piece of chicken", as Chris Rock says. I neglected myself and even our daughter at times to make sure he was satisfied and pleased. Even though deep in my heart I knew he didn't appreciate my efforts, I continued trying. Not only did I continue trying, but I tried harder each and every time. Eventually, he did tell me that no matter what I did it was not good enough.

We live in a world where we want to be loved and we want to love. We also want pleasure and we want to please others. This is a problem that an overwhelming number of people have. The problem is we aim to please. We want to please others to the point of becoming people-pleasers. If you are a people pleaser and you suffer from the disease to please then this section is definitely for you. Trying to please others will rob you of so much of your life.

If you have not already, at some point in your life, you will realize that you lived more for others as opposed to living for yourself. You may have passed up on opportunities and let go of dreams because you tried to keep someone happy. All of these dreams, goals, aspirations, and opportunities were all at the expense of you! My question to you is, are you living for yourself or are you living to please others?

I know what it is like to live for pleasing others. To those of you who know what it's like, or you are presently living to please others; you are living a life that is not aligned with your divine purpose. I am almost positive that if you are living your life pleasing others, you have questioned your purpose in life. You may be asking yourself on a daily basis, how did my life get this way? How did I end up in this situation?

How Do We Fall Into the People Pleasing Trap So Easily?

One of the most common reasons we fall into the trap of wanting to please others is that we ourselves are looking for love and acceptance. No, it's not a bad thing to want to be loved and accepted. But it is a bad thing when you make the mistake I made. I somehow forgot about God's love for me. I was so wrapped up in all of the sweet nothings my abuser whispered and all of the poetry he wrote to me that I forgot about the greatest love of all. That is the love of God. I now realize that even though I was not being treated right by my abuser, I still feared being rejected. I had been rejected by my mother numerous times as a child and even as an adult. I learned at an early age that it is much easier to try to please someone to get their love than to do the right thing. I thought if I loved more, gave more of my time, money, body, or whatever I had to give that the major players in my life would love me in return. I also didn't realize that the opinion God has of me is much more valuable and meaningful than the opinions of those who I expected to love me in return.

We all seek approval and acceptance from the people we love. Too often we place our worth in the hands of others and we depend on the approval of others so much that we lose sight of the most important approval of all, our own. We allow other's opinions of us to diminish how much we value ourselves. Are you suffering from approval addiction? This type of addiction can be extremely harmful in your quest to improve your life.

- ❖ Do you agree with someone or your abuser to avoid disagreeing?
- ❖ Do you seek the approval of your abuser before making a decision?

I am talking about decisions you know how to make and questions you know the answer to, yet you still feel compelled to get the approval of your abuser. This type of behavior causes you to become less reliant on your own judgments, intuition, thoughts, emotions, and over all decision making process. You become less in tune with what is best for you.

Although it is nice to have the support of other people, the only person that can make you fully and wholly happy is you. However, I do understand that one of the many tactics abusers use is to make their victim become dependent on them. We can fall into this approval trap, and not realize it until our self-esteem and self- worth has been diminished. You can begin to change this behavior by not worrying about what other people think about you.

I grew up in a highly dysfunctional family where there were absolutely no boundaries. I learned at an early age that I didn't have any rights, and I allowed everyone to run me over for fear of being punished. My mother didn't respect anyone or their boundaries. We weren't allowed to have an opinion. If we expressed our opinion, she automatically labeled your opinion as being disrespectful to her. As a result, emotional, verbal, physical, and spiritual abuse was rampant in our home. Once I got older there was financial abuse because I thought I could buy my mother's love. My mother didn't allow me to speak up for myself or even disagree with her. If I did speak up for myself to someone else, my mother would take that person's side against me leaving me feeling dejected and unworthy of her support. As a child, I couldn't understand why my mother was nice to me in front of others and publicly praised me yet, behind closed doors treated me awful. I suffered from very low self-esteem over the years as a result of growing up with the abuse from the woman who birthed me. As I got older, I tried unsuccessfully a few times to assert myself with my mother. I have now learned that even though she is my mother, the best contact is no contact because in the end I need to love and protect me.

Like all abusers, she feared that I would tell people about how she really was behind closed doors. She vowed to make my life a living hell, and that is exactly what she has done for over 10 years. I was prime real estate for my husband to pick up where my mother left off. My mother would insult me in front of him thinking he would no longer want to be with me.

She would always use this tactic as a way to run away any boyfriends or close friends. I guess looking back he knew he could get away with abusing me. If I didn't stand up to my mother, why would I stand up to him, and the way his parents treated me. My mistake was confiding in his parents about the way my mother treated me with the hope of being loved by them. That was a big mistake. They later used all of the information I shared with them against me.

Once I became an adult and left my childhood home, I would say to my husband, "I just don't understand it. How can a mother be so rotten to her children?" I couldn't blame her behavior towards me on drugs or alcohol. I was completely baffled. Especially, because we don't dare discuss or talk about mental illness in most black families, so I didn't dare entertain that idea. It wasn't until my husband began to physically abuse me that I began to go on a quest to understand how two people could be so much alike.

I knew I was the common denominator of both of these situations. I wanted to find out what was wrong with me. What did I do to cause the 2 people who should have loved me the most treat me worse than anyone else on this earth. I have had other people not treat me well but so what. They weren't major players in my life so it didn't matter.

I am not a licensed therapist to diagnose anyone. But what I am sure of is what I have experienced with my husband and my mother over many years. During my journey to understand me, I learned that I was a people pleaser, had low self-esteem as a result of being molested at 9 years old, and not supported by my mother. I learned about the characteristics and traits of narcissistic mothers.

My jaw dropped at the similarities of what I had experienced from a child into adulthood from my own mother and descriptions in the various books I was reading. It was like all of the literature I read on the types of mothers was based on the things my mother has said and done to me over the years. As you have already learned, narcissistic abuse strips away your self-confidence leaving you open to feeling like you are just a shell of what you used to be.

Creating and enforcing boundaries are a great way to teach people how you want and need to be treated. It is okay to say, "No." You don't have to agree with everything someone says or does. Abusers hate boundaries. If you set up unwavering firm boundaries in the beginning of a relationship or courtship, an abuser won't stick around. You will be viewed as hard work. He will quickly realize that he can't control you or abuse you. This will save you time, money, heartache, and possibly your life.

Some abusers are very charming and manipulative. They will test you along the way to see how far you will go to please them. People are always going to ask you to do things for them because after all, people need people. This is a part of life. However, when it comes to toxic and abusive people they have no boundaries, and they have a strong sense of entitlement.

Their attitude is what's yours is mine and what's mine is mine. They will often ask you for money no matter what the amount is, ask you to make commitments you are not comfortable with, or take up your time by making you wait only for them not to show up. Abusive people hunt for victims to prey on. As my abuser would tell me, he studied me. He explained to me how he knew me better than I knew myself. He knew that when I said no, I would feel worse than if I would have agreed to something I didn't want to do.

We would have counseling sessions with the pastor from the church we were attending. I would highly suggest if you are going to get counseling individually or as a couple, contact someone who is professionally trained and licensed to conduct therapy sessions. I explained to the pastor that my abuser's mother would use the emergency key to our home and always show up unannounced. She would also come to our home and "go grocery shopping" in our home in addition to always asking for money.

She would take household items, cleaning products, and my personal toiletries and clothing. She was always looking in our cabinets, pantry, and closets for something "new." I explained right in front of my abuser that no one should be allowed to do these things. The pastor asked him if this was happening and my abuser replied, "Yes, that is the kind of relationship I have with my mother. She can have anything of mine she wants." The pastor quoted some scriptures, and told him that his mother was out of order.

The pastor explained to him that his mother should respect me as the woman of the house, and ask me for whatever it is she wanted. I explained how she is always rude to me and only calls me if she wants something. Therefore we didn't have that kind of open relationship to just come and take things without asking. In my opinion, if we have that kind of close relationship, I don't mind at all.

I wish I would have known back then about creating and enforcing boundaries with people who feel entitled, and how to assert myself in a way for it to stop. There were no boundaries. I was accused of being sensitive or playing the victim role. There is nothing worse than knowing you have 5 bottles of dish detergent, and you go to reach for a bottle and there is only one left. Or you are in the middle of preparing dinner, and realize one of the major ingredients is missing.

Unfortunately, as women we like to nurture, love, and "fix" the men in our life to make them feel better. We also want to heal them from the wounds of their past. We listen to their past hurts and somehow want to prove to them that we would never do to them what their previous loves did. I would constantly tell my abuser that it is not fair for other people to be reckless with their finances and then look to us as a financial bailout. There are many issues with this. If you are constantly bailing someone out, they have no incentive to change or do better. You are an enabler. The other major issue is, if we are constantly bailing others out, "Who will bail us out in the event of an emergency?" I always found myself saying, "I feel like I am on an island by myself. What was the point in getting married if you were going to abandon one child and not be there for the wife and child you live with?"

So often we as women think when we hear the phrase, "I'm a mama's boy!" Or "He's a mama's boy!" that we somehow must have found "Mr. Right." WRONG! This is a serious red flag that you learned about in Chapter

3. These types of men will completely drain you physically, spiritually, emotionally, and financially. He will expect you to play the role of his wife and mother.

As a result, we fall into this people pleasing over-commitment coma. We have to start getting into the habit of practicing the terrible twos. That is, get in the habit of saying "No" more often, especially if certain commitments are going to disrupt your life or affect your finances. Even though you want to be nice or do the "right" thing, you have to listen to your inner voice. You have to do what is best for you and your sanity. Let's face it, no matter how much you do or how far you bend over backwards, abusers don't care. They only care about what they want and what they can get. Your well being is not a priority or even on their list of priorities.

There are many different ways your self-esteem can be negatively impacted. Abusers can detect when a woman has low self-esteem. Most abusers will play the knight in shining armor role to rescue you out of a crisis situation as a way to win you over. In my case, I was running like hell from my mother. Once they have won you over, the abuser will begin to test your boundaries. They will start with something small, yet offensive to see how much you will take.

After a while, the testing of boundaries will be greater until the abuser knows for sure you won't leave the relationship. If you don't create boundaries the abuser will take complete advantage of you in the name of love. These experiences can be harmful and damaging to your self-esteem. It is important to know what they are and be able to identify them, so you can protect yourself.

Here are a few examples of what can happen if you don't have a clear set of boundaries and cause of a lack of boundaries:

- ❖ Being bullied by an older person or older relative
- ❖ Your abuser allowing other people to abuse you verbally, physically, financially, or emotionally
- ❖ Finding yourself the target of abuse in your home, church, school, or job
- ❖ Suffered a loss of a significant relationship, job, marriage, or loved one

- Being rejected
- Not having proper love and support during your childhood
- Having a distorted body image
- Not feeling socially acceptable
- Physical changes in your appearance that can cause you to feel bad about yourself
- Experiencing stress such as death, illness, low performance in work, or some other area of your life
- Feeling inadequate
- Not feeling validated
- Feeling like you are not enough
- Feeling like you are not good enough
- It's okay to say NO
- Learn to say no. Don't allow someone to force you to do something you don't want to do.
- Don't be tricked into going back or taking your abuser back
- Not taking time for yourself
- Feeling obligated to agree with your abuser for fear of further abuse
- Not disclosing how you feel about the treatment you are receiving
- Doing things your abuser wants you to do even though you disagree and don't want to participate in the activity
- Go above and beyond a situation in an attempt to prove your loyalty to your abuser
- Taking on the responsibility of people you are not responsible for
- Losing contact with the people who genuinely care about you and your well-being

Take some time to write down ways you can begin to create healthy boundaries in your life. You will have a page for each area you need to create, strengthen, and enforce your boundaries. For each section write down behavior you will accept from others and behaviors that are unacceptable. Also write down how you will address the unacceptable behavior for each category. If you need additional pages, you can finish writing in the Notes section in the back of the book.

For example:

If someone insults me, calls me names, or threatens me, I will no longer pursue a relationship with them. This applies to friendships and romantic relationships.

If I catch someone in a lie, I immediately end the relationship.

If someone asks for money I either say a firm "no", or make sure it is not more than I can afford to lose.

Emotional Boundaries

✳ To be responsible for my own emotions and feelings not someone elses
  - I can empathise but I cannot change the way someone else is feeling
  - It is important to address my feelings when necessary.

✳ I like to help others and will offer my advice but in the future I will explain they must access what they need not me.

✳ If someone has negative feelings that is their issue not mine.

✳ I am only responsible for myself.

Financial Boundaries

✳ My money is mine, no one else's!

✳ I will allow people to borrow cash from me but only if I have it and they will pay it back.

✳ The only person that access to my bank, credit card, overdrafts or catalogue accounts is me and my spending habits is my business.

✳ What I earn is my business, no one else's.

Physical Boundaries

Personal Space
  new people - handshake
  acquaintances - handshake
  friend - hugs
  family - hugs/peck
  Romantic partner - hug/kiss

\#1 I have the right to privacy, when I want it.
- Showering/washing
- dressing/undressing
- toileting
- Being alone, my own space
- Locking the front door
- Closing the curtains
- Telling people to leave when I want them too.
- Leaving when I want to.

Sexual Boundaries

* No means no
* If I feel uncomfortable, stop!
* Only do the things I want to do
* During the dating period, after 3 months, will I have any sexual contact/intercourse with someone.
* Where I feel comfortable having sex.
* Refuse to engage in sexting/pictures.

Spiritual Boundaries

\# I do not believe in God.

\# I am Superstitious

\# I believe in nurturing your soul and inner strength and it will guide you.
(look after yourself).

CHAPTER 7

Ask Questions

"If you never reach out for help, you will continue to deprive yourself." ~Beverly Engel

---

The fourth step in the SPEAK formula is Ask questions. You may know you need help from someone other than your abuser. You know you need to ask questions but you are afraid. You love your abuser. You don't want him to get in trouble, and you feel like you are stuck between a rock and a hard place. If this man loved you as much as you love him, he wouldn't be abusing you in any form. Put yourself first. Get on the phone and call the National Domestic Violence Hotline at 1-800-799-SAFE (7233).

Allow them to assist you. They are there to help you. They can also connect you with your local women's domestic violence shelter. They have an abundance of resources that can be of great wealth for you. Make sure you have a pen and paper to take notes or takes notes on your phone. Whatever the case, be sure to take good notes to reference for later.

This is a very intense time for you and even with the best memory you may not be able to remember all of the valuable information you receive. Make sure you are in a safe place when you call. You don't want to call in the presence of your abuser, or if your abuser could possibly overhear your conversation.

Fear can be very stifling along with the shame and embarrassment that comes along with being abused. These places are confidential, and you can feel safe sharing your information. The more you share with them, the more they will be able to help you. You have to push forward and get to the other side of fear. Don't be afraid to breakthrough to the freedom of being safe for you and your children. Set aside the shame, fear, guilt, and the feeling of vulnerability and reach out for help.

The best thing you can do for yourself and your child(ren) is to contact the National Domestic Violence Hotline or professionals who are trained with helping women who are in domestic violence situations. This organization helped me tremendously. You can call anytime and to talk as well as find out the name of the closest Domestic Violence women's shelter or organization that can help you and support you as you determine what major life decisions are best for you. You make the decision regarding your life and future.

No one else can make this decision for you. I say this because I was at such a low and broken place after the physical abuse. I wanted someone to swoop in and save me. I wanted someone to fix it. I wanted someone to turn back the hands of time. I felt like I didn't have the strength to keep moving forward. I wanted to wave a magic wand so I could at least get the pre-surgery husband back.

During my journey of trying to escape my abuser, I found out many women's shelters are oftentimes full. This was the case when I fled with no plan in the middle of the night with our daughter. However, there is still hope for help and healing. I was disheartened to learn that there are more animal shelters in the United States than there are shelters for women and children of domestic violence.

I knew I needed to reach out for help. It took me a long time to do this. When I finally got the courage to speak up, I confided in my abuser's cousin and his wife. I assumed because they were educators that I could at least be aware of the situation just in case someone found me dead or I went missing. The reaction from the both of them was appalling. They began to choke and punch each other and laugh saying, "See, I can choke her and she won't do anything back. I can punch him in the leg and he won't do anything".

They thought what I told them was some kind of joke, and I was in shock. A week prior to telling them about the abuse, I asked them not to make jokes about his colostomy bag. I had just explained that it was a sensitive topic, and to please not make fun of his colostomy bag in any kind of way. The last time we were with them, they made fun of his colostomy bag. While we were face to face with them, he joined in with their laughter. However, when we got home he took his anger out on me verbally and physically.

On another occasion, we saw a different cousin at a local breakfast restaurant. His cousin came over to our table smiling and greeted my abuser saying, "Hey what's up there Shitbag Johnson." Once again my abuser laughed, and talked with his cousin as if there was nothing wrong. The moment we got home the abuse came full force. He ranted about his cousin's medical procedure that had also gone bad. He talked about all of the things he should have said to his cousin to insult him about the injury to his buttocks.

He said he was angry with himself that he didn't say anything back. He went on a rant about he hated his cousin and hated his colostomy bag. He told every bad thing about this cousin that he knew. Somehow, based on his behavior, I was not surprised by any of the things he said his cousin had done. It took days to try to calm him down after this encounter. It got to the point where I never knew what would set him off.

In most cases, you have been isolated from your family and friends. In rare cases, you may have a relationship with your abuser's family. No matter what the case is, have a clear understanding of who will support you and who won't support you. This is a very difficult thing to do and it is way easier said than done. The people you think will support you may, not and the people you think won't support just may.

If you are blessed enough to have genuine and supportive family and friends listen to them if they are urging you to get out safely. Getting out safely plays an important part of escaping your abuser alive. Leaving your abuser, and after you have left is the most dangerous time. Please don't attempt to leave on your own without having a good solid safe exit strategy plan. Your local women's domestic violence shelter can help you with putting together not only your plan to leave for good, but also provide tips on how to stay alive until you can leave your abuser for good.

Being abused is very overwhelming, and it can cause a severe amount of emotional stress. I grew up in a culture that believed you didn't go to a therapist. The stigma attached to seeing a therapist was awful. The belief was that you didn't tell anyone about your private home issues. There was also the belief that a person was crazy beyond return if they saw a therapist or psychologist. The religious belief was that you got on your knees and told God all about your problems.

I am not saying don't tell God all about your problems, but what I am saying is there is absolutely nothing wrong with seeking professional psychological help if you need to. It is okay to talk to someone who is unbiased and will listen to you without judgment. If we sprain our ankle, have a stomach ache, a cold, ear infection, or some physical bodily ailment we go to the doctor to get it checked out. We want to get it fixed and healed. The same is true for our emotions. The abuse you have endured needs to be repaired and healed by a nonjudgmental professional.

Below are some questions you can ask, and resources that can be provided to you by your local women's domestic violence shelter or the National Domestic Violence Hotline. Describe your situation to determine what options are best for you and your children if you have any.

- Do you need to obtain a restraining order?
- What resources are there for child care?
- Get a physical exam. Ask about free medical care or low-cost medical care that may be available for you and your children.
- Resources to obtain new job skills
- Resources for gaining employment
- Resources for temporary or permanent housing

❖ Some states have crime victim compensation programs for victims of domestic violence

❖ Ask for the names of local attorneys that specialize in domestic violence cases

❖ Ask for the names of therapists or counselors that specialize in working with survivors or victims of domestic

If you feel alone and need support please know that you are not alone. Please contact the National Domestic Violence Hotline at 1-800-799-SAFE (7233).

CHAPTER 8

Keep Your Information Safe

"If we don't protect what we have, it will be destroyed." ~Unknown

---

Keep your information and important documents safely hidden from your abuser.

We have now come to the fifth and final step in the SPEAK Formula. K stands for Keeping your information safe, keeping important documents safe, and keeping an emergency bag packed with important documents and other items you may need. Keep the bag in a safe place where you can access it quickly. Some of these documents and items can be kept in a small lock box or in a large envelope. Just make sure they are together in one safe place hidden from your abuser.

You may want to keep the information in a safety deposit box, with a trusted friend, a trusted family member, a trusted neighbor, or with someone you can trust outside of the home. Oftentimes, women flee their homes with just the clothes on their back.

If you can, pack an overnight bag filled with clothing and other necessities. Keep it in the trunk of your car at all times. The following suggestions are not a guarantee that you will have a smooth transition or financial security. However, they do play an important role in helping you to plan safely as you prepare to escape.

The following documents are an important part of your planning. If you do not already have some of these documents, make it your business to get them. The reason why is because sometimes we have to leave our home in a hurry. A high percentage of women leave home with no money. Although some of these documents are public records, there are sometimes fees applied in order to obtain the documents.

You have a divine purpose and you weren't created to be abused by anyone. No one can tell you to stay with your abuser or to leave your abuser. Ultimately, that is your decision. My hope for you is that you make up your mind that you and/or your children are worth more and act on that knowledge in a safe way. You deserve a better life.

If you don't have your own individual personal checking or savings account, I highly suggest you get one. Make sure your abuser knows nothing about your individual accounts. Have the account set up so that you get paperless online statements that go to an email address that only you have access to. This way there is not a paper trail coming to your home.

I understand your funds may be limited. I also understand you may not be able to run to the bank to make frequent deposits. If your situation will allow, you can save what I call "couch change." Start saving the change you get from the grocery store, or whenever you get change back. However, it is very important to save every penny you have, or can get your hands on. This is especially critical if your abuser controls all of your money.

If you have a green/immigration card, make sure you keep it in a safe place. In most situations, abusers will threaten to take it away or hide it from you. If this is the case, you may want to get a replacement card that the abuser knows nothing about. This also applies to any other documents or identification cards you may need regarding your immigration status or ability to work and earn an income.

Your jewelry may play an important role in your survival. No, I am not saying run out and sell it. What I am saying is that even though your jewelry may have sentimental value it may also serve as a resource to plan a new future. Either way, make sure you take your jewelry with you.

If you have important documents such as life insurance policies, health insurance policies, payment books for your mortgage, car payments, lease or rental agreements; and there is only one copy, and you don't want to tip off your abuser make copies of these documents.

You may or may not be planning on it at the time to file a civil protection order or restraining order. When you do decide to pursue this, you want to make sure you have a photo of your abuser as well as your abuser's social security number.

I know in the digital age we keep everything on our digital devices. Back - up your files, make copies, and I would also suggest you keep important phone numbers and contact information written on a piece of paper also hidden with these documents. Just in case your abuser destroys your phone or electronic device.

You will need your photo identification if you decide to stay at the local women's shelter, get your own apartment, purchase your own home, and overall to conduct business that will lead to living a new life safe from abuse.

Here is a list of some of items you can pack:

- Checkbook
- Green/Immigration Card
- Work permit
- VISA & Immigration Paperwork
- Jewelry
- Bank Card
- Credit Card
- Life Insurance Policies
- Child Custody papers
- Mortgage Information/Payment Book
- Lease, Rental Agreement, or Deed to Home

- Civil Protection Order/Restraining Order/Protection From Abuse
- Birth Certificates (you and your child/children)
- Address Books
- Photo of Abuser
- Baby Items (diapers, food, medication, favorite toy)
- Car Keys
- Money
- Passport
- Public Assistance/Welfare ID
- Mobile Phone/Coins to use in a payphone
- Driver's License
- Car Registration
- Car Insurance
- Divorce papers
- Health Insurance Cards
- Medical Records
- Social Security Card
- Your Spouse/Partner's Social Security Number
- Important Legal Documents
- Police Records/Reports
- Medications for you and your children
- Items for baby/children (medication, diapers, non-perishable food, milk, favorite toy or blanket)
- Medical/Immunization Records for Children
- School Records For Children
- Clothing
- Eyeglasses

- ❖ Inhaler
- ❖ House keys – keep a spare in the car, with a trusted friend or neighbor
- ❖ Photos or any items of sentimental value

Use the next page to write down a list of all of the items you will need, so you can begin gathering and organizing what you need.

Important Documents

_____
_____
_____
_____
_____
_____
_____
_____
_____
_____
_____
_____
_____
_____
_____
_____
_____
_____

CHAPTER 9

Making the Transition: Did I Do the Right Thing? Maybe I Shouldn't Have Left.

"And the day came when the risk to remain tight in a bud was more painful than the risk it took to blossom." ~Anais Nin

---

You may now be at the point of your journey where you have gathered the courage and strength to speak up and get out of your abusive relationship. You find yourself once again at another critical point in your life. The actions you take in the days, weeks, and months' following your separation from your abuser lays the foundation for the rest of your life. It is at this crossroad in your life to decide whether or not you will value your self-worth, or discount your self-worth and self-respect and donate it to the proverbial local thrift shop.

If you made the decision to have the courage to end your relationship with your abuser, you are experiencing a flood of different emotions. Initially, you may be feeling liberated, empowered, and relieved. Then suddenly you feel all sorts of unwanted emotions for leaving. You may feel guilt, fear, anxious, sad, shame, afraid, sorrow, panic, doubt, and remorse. These feelings can be so overwhelming that you may contemplate going back.

Your surroundings may have changed. Your environment may have changed. You may have left physically or you are physically out of the abusive relationship. But your heart, mind, and soul is still with that man. These are some of things no one really talks about. Everyone from family, friends, coworkers, and neighbors will be quick to tell you, "Just leave!". I am here to tell you that leaving is just as painful as, or even more painful than enduring the abuse. At least with the abuse, we know if we say just the right things we may be able to avoid making him angry.

We know we have a roof over our head. We know we have financial security even if we don't control the money. But once you leave your mind, body, and soul will be exposed to a new element that is free from abuse. It is almost like a shock to your system. You may even feel like you would be better off if you went back. You now have time to grieve, and because of this, all of the emotional pain that you may not have dealt with comes rushing in.

You begin to think of all of things you could change. You think of all of the maybes, the whys, what ifs, should haves, could haves, and would haves as to how you and your abuser can work things out and be together again. I know you are struggling with shame and guilt and wondering if you made the right decision. Your focus needs to be on loving yourself. Don't allow the need to be loved or feel loved by someone else compromise your safety. Don't allow someone else's insecurities cause you to neglect yourself.

Reality has set in that you are now alone. Your life no longer revolves around your abuser. You feel like you have a gaping hole in your broken heart. Your routine has changed. Your abnormal is no longer normal. You are in an uncomfortable place in life. You feel like you have been jolted into another dimension. You may even feel like you need a "fix" from your abuser because you have been addicted to the dysfunction of abuse.

You are going to second guess yourself, and question whether or not you made the right decision because the painful pain that you are feeling is so doggone painful. Your mind will have thoughts of what your abuser is doing, is he happy, is he thinking about you. I know from experience, it is much easier to say than actually doing. Don't worry about your abuser.

Focus on you and your children and making a better life. Trust me when I say, "Your abuser is most likely not thinking of you!" He has moved on to his next targets (most abusers live double lives and have multiple targets). In my case, my abuser only thought of me long enough to inflict more emotional harm via social media.

Having all of these mixed emotions is completely normal. Let's face it, your relationship was not all bad with your abuser. I am sure you had very good times, and he did have some good traits which is why you remained in the relationship. Oftentimes, even when the bad behavior creeps in for long periods of time, we continue to stay searching for a glimpse of the good to come back.

Use the anger, hurt, pain, and courage you used to walk away as fuel to stay away. Your abuser won't change unless he wants to change. You can't make him treat you the way he treats other people. The bottom line is for whatever reason he does not respect you, and if he does not respect you he won't protect you. Your feelings of wanting to go back are because your abuser has brainwashed you into believing you can't make it on your own.

This is what is called a Trauma Bond. You were once a strong independent woman before you met your abuser. Now you have a difficult time making a decision without your abuser's approval no matter how major or minor it is. Who you are has been slowly eroded over a period of time without you even realizing it.

That person you once knew yourself to be seems to no longer exist. You may be questioning yourself as to why or how you would allow someone to take so much of who you are away from you. Trauma bonds are created when we begin to agree and identify with our abuser to avoid some form of punishment. As time goes by, and you have been isolated from the outside world, the environment the abuser creates becomes the norm. Trauma bonds sometimes have women so brainwashed into believing they deserve the abuse they are getting that they are emotionally frozen and can't leave the relationship.

Escaping the Trauma Bond causes massive guilt. Your goal is to overcome the guilt and know the abuse is not your fault. You are not to blame for someone else's actions. You may have feelings of blaming yourself for the things your abuser shouldn't have done. You may be questioning yourself. Why did I speak up? If I had just kept my mouth shut, he wouldn't have beaten me.

After my husband began to physically abuse me, I questioned myself everyday wondering if he would ever stop. I had finally learned about the National Domestic Violence Hotline and local domestic violence women's shelter from a brochure a policeman handed to me on one of their visits. I refused to look at it initially because I kept saying to myself and to the policeman, this is not my husband, he just had a bad surgery.

I kept thinking to myself, "I am not that woman who is lying to protect her abuser." I was in fact that woman. I finally dialed the numbers on the brochure, and I would call a few times during the day because I wanted to get a different answer to my question. I wanted to know if once my husband started beating me if he would ever stop or change. Each time I would call and ask this same question, someone from the hotline or the local women's shelter would tell me the same answer, "It will only get worse." I spoke to woman who told me I am lucky to be alive. I didn't realize the importance of getting to the hospital after being choked. She explained to me that sometimes women who are strangled during a violent encounter such as mine can die up to four hours after being strangled. Hearing these words made me shake as I thought about how I passed out as he sat on top of me choking me. As he banged my head against the floor all I could see was a very bright silver light before I blacked out.

I was in so much emotional pain, and I felt so much guilt for calling the police, filing the protection order, and seeing him go to jail. I felt in my heart that I had made the right decision but the pain of the process made me feel like maybe I should have hung in there a little longer to see if he would have changed back to being non-physically abusive.

Some days I felt like he enjoyed seeing how he had stolen something from the pit of my soul after he would beat me. I sometimes miss the good times we shared but I don't miss the fear and intimidation. I don't miss the constant reminder of him letting me know what he could physically do to me. I still have moments where I am in just as much pain now as I was when this first started. When you get to the point of your journey where you are in the midst of the healing process you will begin to turn that corner and begin to regain your strength again.

As I discussed in an earlier chapter, leaving an abuser is the most dangerous time for a woman who is escaping a domestic violence situation. This is when most women who leave are murdered. You have to be aware of your surroundings. You also have to keep in mind; now that you are gone your abuser is angry.

My abuser could be fuming mad, but he had a way of remaining frighteningly calm. If your abuser contacts you wanting to meet, don't disclose your location. Don't meet with your abuser. He may only be acting nice to get you in his presence to harm you. If for any reason you have to meet, contact your attorney or the local police department and ask for an escort. Protecting yourself and staying safe after you have escaped with your life is a critical step.

Making the transition to start loving yourself first and meeting your own needs is a difficult task to accomplish. Your life has revolved around pleasing someone else and meeting their needs. You have spent so much time being controlled that you may be having difficulties making decisions. You are in a state of panic and operating from a place of fear because you are questioning whether or not you made the right decision by leaving, filing a protection order, or having him arrested.

These are all things you needed to do to protect yourself. Even though you have been abused and mistreated you still love him, and wish you could be together again. What you are feeling may seem completely irrational. When recovering from this type of abuse, these feelings are normal. You are not any of the negative self talk names you may be calling yourself. You are someone who needs time to heal, know your worth, and recover from the trauma inflicted upon you by your abuser. You are doing the very best that you know how at this point. Be kind to yourself. Don't allow anyone to tell you how you should heal as long as you are not harming yourself or anyone else.

Emotional affects of Abuse

Women who have been in an abusive relationship suffer emotionally from the affects of the abuse they have endured. Children who are abused and/or witness their mother being physically or emotionally abused suffer as well. Dealing with abuse is a heavy burden to try to carry alone. Contact your local women's domestic violence shelter to find out what kind of services they offer.

They may be able to refer you to an adult therapist for you and a children's therapist for your child. My local shelter referred me to an agency that provides services for adults and children who have experienced domestic violence. My local women's shelter also offers a support group for women who are currently in a domestic violence situation, living in the shelter, and women who have escaped their violent situation but still need support. I am sharing this information with you because I didn't know how valuable a local domestic violence women's shelter would be for my survival.

I went to see a therapist because I would shake uncontrollably. I was so nervous that my mouth would dry up to the point where I couldn't move my lips. My abuser would stomp and jerk at me as if he was going to choke me again. He would laugh as I flinched asking me if I was scared and if I thought he was going to choke me or slam me. He found it so amusing, he would have tears in his eyes and laugh saying, "Now see, you are making me cry 'cause boy I swear I can hear your knees knockin.'"

It got to the point that my daughter and I would barricade ourselves in the master bedroom at night to keep him from hurting us as we slept. I went to a therapist because everyone around us was turning a blind eye. On one occasion after he beat me, once again I covered for him and refused to send him to jail. The police took him to his parent's apartment. Shortly after, his mother called me asking me what was going on. At this point, I finally told her what he had been doing to me. She acted as if I said nothing.

Her response was, "He needs his things so he can stay the night with me." I told her they couldn't come to our house without the police because at this point I didn't trust them. She had no empathy, nothing. I got off of the phone, and I packed all of his colostomy supplies, medication, and clothing to make sure he had everything he needed.

He and his mother arrived with the police. His mother saw the redness on my neck, the blood on my shirt, and the broken tray table he hit me with. She didn't ask about my well-being or if our daughter was okay. The only thing she asked was, "Did you pack his things, where are they?" I gave her the bags and she left. I felt worthless. These people over the years had used me, abused me, insulted me, and acted as though I was an outsider for 20 years. I wanted to know what was it about me that would allow someone to treat me in such a degrading manner as if I didn't matter.

It wasn't until I began to see a therapist that I started to learn that my self-esteem and self-worth had been eroded beginning with growing up in an abusive dysfunctional home. It is a common pattern for a girl who has been molested at a young age and endured abuse to grow up and enter into an intimate relationship with an abuser. We identify with what is familiar to us. My abuser's behavior and the behavior of his parents were familiar to me. They were doing the same things to me that my own mother had done to me knowingly and intentionally. I take full responsibility because I confided in them about the abusive things my mother had done to me as a child and even in adulthood.

My mother also acted out in front of my abuser so why wouldn't he think he could do the same thing. I confided in his mother telling her about the abuse I endured from my mother. Instead of embracing me, she used the information against me and manipulated me into allowing her to have a sense of entitlement and no boundaries. I no longer wanted to be a door mat. I wanted to see a therapist, so someone could teach me how to stand up for myself.

I found out that the things my abuser and his parents were telling me I was being too sensitive about was their way of bullying me into doing things I didn't want to do. Seeing a therapist can be highly beneficial. Not only do you learn about others, but more importantly you learn about yourself.

I was embarrassed because I had a psychology degree but I was so beaten down emotionally that I couldn't put a label on what I was experiencing. I felt so liberated when I was able to tell my therapist what was happening in my life. My therapist would listen attentively and let me know the terms, labels, and names of the different things I was experiencing or had experienced over the years including those experiences with my mother. I was in shock and heartbroken at the same time to be told that I was being abused for 20 years by my abuser and all my life by my own mother.

I was initially told by the legal advocate at the shelter that I was being abused and I immediately disagreed with her saying, "Just the past few months he turned life threatening violent towards me because of his surgery." The legal advocate explained that I didn't have to be physically abused to be abused. I didn't realize verbal, emotional, financial, and spiritual abuse was abuse because of the environment I had grown up in. I also didn't view his poking me, shoving me, grabbing me by the arm or ear, or forcing me to have sex as abuse because it was not life threatening to me. Once again I was in denial.

By the time I got to my therapist, and she showed me the Domestic Violence Power Wheel, it was then that I realized I had indeed been abused for 20 years. I knew what I was going through didn't feel good, but it never donned on me to equate it to abuse. These were some of the things I had grown up with and believed to be normal as a result of having to interact with my "deeply" religious mother. Making the decision to go see a therapist without my abuser sitting in the room intimidating me to make sure I covered up was the most liberating feeling I had ever experienced.

I was no longer a fraud having to pretend I had the perfect husband or perfect mother. I no longer had the pressure of feeling like I couldn't make a mistake. I no longer had to hide the fact that these things were happening in our home. For the first time in my life I felt free to be me. I also felt a deep sadness because I used to tell people I just don't know why my mother is so mean and hateful behind closed doors. I can't blame her behavior towards me on her use of alcohol, drugs, or men because she didn't indulge in any of these things. When I began to pour my heart out to the therapist about my childhood relationship and non-existent adult relationship with my mother, I learned about the Narcissistic Mother. I was angry with myself because I think had I done the work years ago to resolve the issues of why my mother treats me the way she does; I would have seen the warning signs of abuse in my marriage.

Sometimes when we are rejected by one abuser we look for love in all of the wrong places and we become easy prey for the next abuser. We will also accept abuse and tolerate abuse because of our deep desire to be loved by someone else. We have to learn to love ourselves first regardless as to who will or won't love us.

Post Traumatic Stress Disorder or PTSD can develop as a result of being exposed to emotional, verbal, sexual, or physical abuse. Symptoms related to PTSD include the inability to control replaying the events of the abuse over and over in your mind, nightmares, panic attacks, depression, anxiety attacks, and flashbacks of the abuse. If you are experiencing any of these symptoms, I would highly suggest contacting a trained medical professional for help. You are not alone, and there are people who know exactly what you need in order to heal from the wounds of your past.

My abuser would often tell me that I better not ever think about leaving him. I would think about it from time to time but I never acted on the thought because of my fear of being alone. He made it clear that if I ever tried to leave him I would regret it for the rest of my life. He would smile and laugh the entire time of telling me.

He would laugh and say, "I will take half and more than half of what you have if you ever think about leaving me." He would then call out for our daughter to come into the room with us and tell her, "Hey, if your mom was a busted bitch working at the rental furniture store, or the bank making $8.50 an hour, I wouldn't be with her." His favorite thing to tell me was, "If I wasn't secure as a man, Dr. Bitch I wouldn't be with you.

Your shit is tight and you got your stuff together. No man is going to ever step to you because of all of your degrees, and how well put together you are. You are a juggernaut. No one will want you". I had no idea what a juggernaut was the first time he said this. I grabbed my phone and looked it up. My daughter would stand there in disbelief not knowing what to do or say. I could see the embarrassment in her eyes for me.

Some days I still struggle as I feel like no one will ever want me. I used to have the fear of being alone but I no longer have that fear anymore. I actually enjoy being in my own company. It was very hard at first, but I have learned to embrace it. I thought if I was transparent and I did everything he asked me to do, that he would love me in return. It turns out the more I did for him the worse he treated me. I have now come to the point where I love that I love loving me for who I am.

I told myself I didn't want to be the kind of woman we are all too familiar with. You know the kind of woman I am talking about. The kind of woman I am growing out of. I was so emotionally broken that I felt like I had to have a man in my life even if he was no good for me. We all know this woman. She is trying to fill an empty emotional void in her life. It is most likely the result of a childhood trauma. As broken women, we sometimes attract abusive men and settle because we have a longing to feel whole and complete. Instead of paying attention to the red flags, we are flattered that someone is paying us some kind of attention. We shouldn't allow anyone to define our value or dictate our worth. There comes a time when we need to be responsible and accountable for our own emotional, financial, spiritual, and physical security.

Gone will be the days we feel like a scared child, a lost lamb, or needing to be validated by someone else. As we learn from our experience and heal from the abuse, we will become strong and secure in who we are as women - who are more than capable of caring for ourselves when we need to. It is your choice, you can choose to be in an unsafe place, or you can choose to protect yourself and/or your children. You can decide whether you want to stay a victim, or if you want to survive and thrive.

You may be wondering what you can do to get beyond the point of feeling like your heart is still with him even though your mind says run like hell. You may be having thoughts of returning to your abuser. I am not saying relive everything that your abuser has done to you, but what I am saying is: think about how you felt when you were with your abuser.

I would sometimes block out the bad things. I had to force myself to think about the bad things, and what I felt or how I felt. This quickly gave me the strength to keep moving forward in a new direction in life free from my abuser. Here are some other strategies you can use to stay free from your abuser. These are forms of what is called No Contact. No contact refers to not having any form of communication with your abuser for the purpose of healing and staying safe.

- ❖ Not accepting your abuser's phone calls
- ❖ No texting
- ❖ No talking on the phone
- ❖ No contact via social media
- ❖ Get a new telephone number
- ❖ Not allowing him to just show up to your home or job (announced or unannounced)
- ❖ Change your phone number
- ❖ Get a new email address
- ❖ Not allowing family or friends to relay messages from your abuser to you

Implementing the method of No Contact is very difficult. I am not going to tell you it is easy. It's like going on a strict diet, kicking a bad habit, or being told you can't indulge in your favorite guilty pleasure. Self-discipline is a key component of freeing yourself from your abuser. You may be asking yourself, "How can I walk away from a relationship I have invested so much in? Or "How do I move on when my heart is breaking.?"

You have to decide that knowing you are worth more is greater than the pain of being abused. So many times we break up and make up and each time is worse than the last. It gets to the point where all you can focus on is when the next break up is going to happen. Breaking the cycle of domestic violence is up to you. He will continue his abusive behavior for as long as you allow him to come back. The decision to leave or cut off all contact is not necessarily the hard part. The tough part of this process is leaving safely and staying gone. I am talking not having contact with him and affording him the opportunity to sweet talk you into coming back home or vice versa. Remember, his "I miss you" is not genuine if he is physically, verbally, or emotionally abusing you.

Live With No Regrets

On my journey I have come to embrace not living with regrets. While in the midst of a storm I couldn't understand exactly why something was happening, but eventually I realized things happen for a reason. Everything that happens to us is sometimes happening for us. I had to stop looking at my situation as something horrible. I now understand that if these things wouldn't have happened to me I wouldn't be on a mission to help other women. I wouldn't have gained the wisdom, or grown, or become a stronger person.

Don't get caught up with your perceived limitations. Think big and work hard to rebuild yourself. As you step up the ladder of progress, you will just about find out that the impossible has just become a little bit more possible. Perhaps one of the biggest stumbling blocks in healing from an abusive relationship is past regrets. Too many times we become so obsessed with all of the times in the past when we were unable to speak up or do things differently. Our goal is to believe we are not doomed to fail as a survivor.

What actually happens is that we "program" ourselves to fail. We are still living in the past, unable to break away from the "failure chain" that links us to our past selves and past life. We punish ourselves, and we doom ourselves to repeating the same old mistakes over and over again. In order to do things differently, we must learn to be different. Our thoughts, actions, and attitudes must all be different than they were in the past. One big way to be different is in the way we perceive our mistakes.

There's no room in our lives to live with regret. Regret is a waste, and it does nothing to enhance who you. In reality, all it does is feed on you. Regret will bleed you dry emotionally, physically, spiritually, and financially. If you want to be free from a life of abuse to achieve your vision and goals and live your life to its fullest potential; you must not allow regret to keep you chained to the past in a prison of "should haves," "could haves," and "would haves."

One of the best ways to loosen the power that regret has on you is to accept your past mistakes. Allow yourself to be human and realize that as a human, you will make mistakes, and that's okay, because that is how you learn and that's how you grow.

But now, let's take it one step further. Not only should you accept your past mistakes - you should embrace them. That's right, be grateful that you are aware of your mistakes. Why in the world should you do that? Because if you are aware that you have made a mistake, then you are also aware that you need to do something different next time around to be successful.

To every action there is an equal and opposite reaction. So you can look at what you did in the past to achieve the wrong results, and use that as your blueprint for what you need to do to achieve the right results. So when those past mistakes come to mind, don't get stuck in regret and allow yourself to follow the same path that caused the mistakes in the first place. Instead, embrace those mistakes, and use them as a valuable learning tool – that my friend will be your roadmap to success.

Take the action you need to take to go in the direction you desire to be. There will be tears, frustration, and pain along your journey but it will be worth once you do what is best for you. You may lose family or friends or some people along the way. If they don't like you anymore, that's okay. Let them know they can't continue on your journey with you.

Stop living someone else's life and create your own story. You will be covered the entire time by your higher power: The Universe, God, Buddha, Allah, Source, or whoever your higher power is does not operate in the realm of fear, chaos, and confusion. In order to take your life to the next level, safe environment, and healthy place you must trust your voice. Do the work and get a sense of calm that it is okay to be yourself.

Get emotionally naked if you have to….and what I mean by that is if you have to cry out to your higher power for strength, then do so! Be very real with yourself about what you are thinking and feeling. Cry until you can't cry anymore. Call out to God and tell Him your needs. Tell Him how bad you are hurting. I got to a point where I no longer asked God to take away my pain. I began to understand that the pain was a part of the process. I then began to ask God to comfort me through the pain. I began to praise Him from the pit to the palace.

Wait On God's Timing

I can remember being in the middle of the divorce, and the pain of everything was almost unbearable. I had joined some support groups, called hotlines, prayer lines, and read every book I could get my hands on looking for answers to how I could ease my pain. I wanted to ease the pain of my husband, my daughter, and turn back the hands of time. I didn't want a divorce. I just wanted for the abuse to stop. I didn't want to deal with his abusive attorney. I was frustrated with the Guardian ad Litem who kept insinuating that the abuse never happened.

I understood all too well, I had been charmed and manipulated by my abuser so I could only be but so frustrated with the Guardian ad Litem for not knowing any better. I would cry out to God asking Him if He could hear me. I wanted to know if He knew the height, depth, and width of my pain. I was stuck. I couldn't imagine living life without the person that I had shared some really good times with.

One woman who was recently divorced advised me to call my attorney and "stop the bleeding". She wanted me to just tell my attorney that I wanted to sign all everything over to him, sign the papers, and walk away so I could begin to heal. Being in a painful divorce is like an open wound that won't stop bleeding. Whatever you are going through don't rush it, slow it, or try to stop it. It's not about our timing. For what happens in our life it is not about our plan that we have mapped out for our life. It is about God's plans, purpose, and timing for what He has planned for our life.

I will tell you my needs have NEVER not been met. My needs have always been met, and so will yours if you just ask. Get comfortable with who is looking back at you in the mirror. Your worth has nothing to do with the number of followers or likes on social media. Before you were created in your mother's womb, you were valuable and worth it and you still are. Each day stay encouraged and don't exist in a state of fear.

Remind yourself to stay focused. Realign yourself with meditation, and in order to break down the barriers of fear, feed your mind with information and knowledge that will get you closer to a better you. When you do this, feelings of liberation and moments of clarity emerge. If you want to get to the other side of fear you have to have faith. Fear and faith can't share the same space. Stand in your worth and own who you are.

Love yourself and respect yourself enough to have the courage to walk away from abuse. Trust your instincts, and listen to that feeling in your gut that says enough is enough. What will it take for you to walk away and stay away? Think about the consequences for when someone does not treat you with respect, love, and care that you deserve.

You have to set clear firm boundaries that say, "You choked me!", "You called me a bitch!", "You cheated on me!", "You stole from me!", "You won't respect my wishes!" These are deal breakers. When these things happen to you, your abuser is telling you that you don't matter to him. It is up to you to say I am worth more, and therefore this relationship is over for good. The days of walking on eggshells are over!

CHAPTER 10

Now That You're On Your Own, Breathe, Grieve, & Be Good to Yourself

"We have a duty not just to give to others, but to give to ourselves – and to see ourselves as worthy of receiving. We have a duty to honor ourselves."
~Patricia Spadaro

I found myself in a fetal position day after day, all day and all night long. Many weekends, I cried all night long. I have had too many sleepless nights to count. I've never felt this depth of pain before in my life. It is such a painful pain. I believe no one should have to ever experience what I call the 3 Deadly D's and especially not in such a short span of time. Initially I was grieving the shock of being a victim of domestic violence. I never wanted to be a victim of anything. I deplore the word victim because I always believed that no matter what life throws my way I would survive.

I didn't want to file for a protection order, and it took me a while before I finally did file for protection. Once he was served with the orders, he went and filed for a divorce the next day. I was devastated again. I was in complete shock that he would file for a divorce. To me, I thought whoa, he would rather get a divorce than stop beating me and terrorizing our daughter.

I thought for sure that he would calm down and realize how his behavior was affecting all of us. I thought we could possibly reconcile if he saw I was serious about wanting him to stop physically abusing me. Over the years, I would think to myself and tell him I don't care what you say about me. I didn't know that I should have cared because the verbal and emotional abuse completely destroyed any sense of self-esteem and self-confidence that I thought I had. Once he filed for the divorce I felt as if I was in a blurred fog. Life was moving so fast yet extremely slow.

He hired an attorney that was so unethical, rude, and nasty. I thought to myself that he must have lied on me to this attorney for someone to be so ruthless. This man attacked my personal character, attempted to intimidate me, and even went as far as to bully my attorney. The lies that he told during the divorce were very hurtful. He manipulated his attorney as well as the Guardian ad Litem. Based on their actions I know within my heart he had to have painted an ugly picture of me by the way I was being treated.

I went into the divorce thinking it was going to be played fairly. The judge even joked, and said I should be an engineer because when she said we needed to decide on how to split our marital property I said, "I don't have a problem with anything he wants to take, he can even have his aunt's plasma TV." I wanted to be as fair as possible. I even told him to bring a moving company to come get whatever he wanted from the house.

He didn't do it because I suggested it. It was also his way of trying to make it seem as though I was keeping him from getting whatever he wanted. As I have already explained, as a survivor of domestic violence, there is a great possibility that you will be further abused by the court system. As the divorce dragged on, life became more and more painful. I had lost 75lbs. Our daughter was still having nightmares. We were afraid to be in the house, yet afraid to leave the house for fear of what he might do to us. The fear of not knowing when he would actually follow through with his threats was emotionally and mentally draining. I missed the man that I had shared great times with. As I have said many times before, it was not all bad. Not a day goes by that I wish he wouldn't have had to have gone through the trauma of such a horrific surgery.

One Friday evening I decided to venture out to get some bottled water with our daughter. The evening felt very heavy. As we left out of the grocery store, the rain was pouring extremely hard. I said to my daughter, "If daddy was here, he would have pulled the car around for us." In that moment I stood there, and I prayed for him as I often did. I asked God to comfort him and ease his pain. I know within my heart that he had to have been hurting. I also thought if it had not been for that awful surgery we wouldn't have been going through all of the madness we were experiencing.

When we returned home from the store, the house alarm made an odd noise that it had never made before when I opened the door. I checked the phone, and I saw where the alarm company and police station left messages. My heart began to immediately pound as I didn't know what to make of the situation. The alarm company informed me that they had spoken to my husband, and he told them that I would take care of having the alarm reset.

I thought it was odd that she had spoken to him because his contact information was no longer on file. I then spoke to the police, and let them know all was well. I still don't know what caused the alarm to go off. Later that night our dog was very restless. He kept whimpering and whining. He also kept running to the kitchen door looking for my husband to come in from the garage. This was always his routine.

Anytime my husband would leave the house and come home Hines, our dog, would run to the door to greet him. This particular night Hines kept running to the door whimpering and whining. He repeated these actions all night long. I didn't get any sleep. I was afraid maybe it was my husband lurking around outside, and the dog could smell him. I found myself at 3AM explaining to a dog that I missed daddy too, but we needed to go to bed. I was heartbroken because even the dog was having a tough time dealing with all of this chaos.

The following evening I decided to check my social media. I saw a familiar photo of a toddler on my timeline that caught my eye. To my surprise, it was my husband in the photo. I was curious as to why someone would have a photo posted of him at that age. I viewed his profile and realized there were messages asking for prayer for him from earlier that day.

Then I finally saw the gut-wrenching posts that said he had passed away. I immediately called his best friend's widow who informed me of his passing. My husband's parents sent his body from the hospital straight to the crematorium without even notifying. Even if no one cared for me, someone could have contacted me or my attorney to have our daughter notified of her father's condition and passing. On Monday morning I contacted several different funeral homes to track down the body. I finally spoke with the funeral home that had possession of the body. I explained to the funeral director that I was not notified of his collapse or death, and I identified myself as his wife. The funeral director explained that he was informed by my husband's parents that my husband was divorced.

I told him I could provide documents that stated otherwise. I explained that the only thing I wanted was for my daughter to have some sort of closure. When I told her of her father's passing she cried and she sobbed, "Now I will never get the answers from him as to why he changed!" I told the funeral director that my daughter wanted to see her father before they cremated him. I also thought it was a good idea for her to see him one last time. I didn't want her to grow up carrying the pain of not being able to see her father for the last time ever.

The funeral director informed me that the attorney was threatening him to the point that he contacted his own attorney. The attorney from the divorce was like a jack of all trades and master of none. He was very good at scare tactics, and trying to bully me into submission but that seemed to be about it.

I stood firm in my trust in God that He would take care of me throughout the entire bitter process. The attorney made threats about if I wanted my abuser's ashes, veteran's flag or anything else, to see him in probate court. I had no idea that I needed to follow-up in probate court. Once I hired a different attorney to file the paperwork for probate court, his attorney made negative slanderous comments about my swift action.

I paid for a private viewing for me and my daughter to see her father's dead body. We didn't attend the services that were later held at the church with his family. I felt like God had the final word. There was nothing more to say to anyone. There was no need to go somewhere we were obviously not welcome.

We didn't receive a call from any of his family members or the pastor and his wife. I was rather surprised with the pastor's actions even though I shouldn't have been considering how he responded to the domestic violence. These people had been to our home numerous times eating our food and having a good time fellowshipping. At the time, I was deeply hurt, feeling dejected, and grieved for some time about it. The worst part of going through something like this back to back and all at once; is that no one called to check on me and our daughter to find out if we were okay or needed anything.

There were no cakes, cookies, pies, or covered dished - there was nothing. Not even from the man of the cloth. No one checked to see if we just needed something as simple as a word of encouragement. I finally realized that God is in control. I realized I didn't needs these people. God knows all, he sees all, and we all have to take responsibility and be accountable for our own actions. No matter how bad things get, no matter who attacks our character, no matter who attacks us physically, spiritually, financially, emotionally, verbally, no matter how grim the situation may seem, just hold on. Always trust in the will of your High Power. Mine is God and I fully surrender and trust Him.

Once I got to probate court. I learned from my attorney that my husband had cancelled the life insurance policies and the one policy he didn't cancel, he left to his mother. These were policies we planned and paid for with our hard earned money. Had I passed away he could have retired on the spot because he was still listed as my beneficiary.

Prior to him filing for the divorce, he went and changed the status on many of his documents. Once I was served with divorce papers, we were ordered by the court not to change any documents including beneficiaries for life insurance policies and retirement accounts. The information on my documents remained the same.

He didn't leave anything for our daughter to secure her future. He changed his paperwork as if our daughter was not a minor that needed to be taken care of. His parents didn't even set up a trust fund for her. She no longer exists to them. They are still angry because she called the police on their baby.

During our marriage, our plan was to make sure if something happened to one of us, the other would be able to take care of our daughter and her college education. Unfortunately, he didn't keep his word or hold up his side of the bargain.

Transitioning from domestic violence to the restraining order, the divorce, and his death made me feel as though I was drowning with no chance of gasping for air. I missed him, and I would reminisce about the good times, our dreams, and goals together. The truth is, I still loved him. I think I always will but just not in a toxic bonded way.

I will always love him as a person and being the father of our beautiful daughter. I was looking for that glimmer of love that we once had. But once Pandora's Box is open, you can never go back. The love you sought from your spouse; you have to give to yourself. Take care of yourself.

You may be feeling that deep dark painful pain that seems unbearable. If so, I want you to lean into the pain and feel the pain, so you can move forward. You can't heal what you conceal. If you hide, deny, or ignore your pain; it will destroy you mentally, physically, spiritually, and emotionally. The emotional pain would sometimes shoot through my body physically. The most important part of healing is to acknowledge your pain. If you have to cry, rant, sing, dance, hit pillows, or write. You must embrace the pain and just breathe and grieve your losses.

My daughter told me when all of this first began, and I was so out of it. It was hard to get my attention. I would be in bed from Friday evening until Monday morning. I only got up to go to the bathroom. I didn't realize it at the time, but I was grieving. You are grieving too. You are grieving the loss of the dreams you once shared, the hopes you had for your marriage, the decisions you made in the past or what you perceive as mistakes.

Don't confuse your grief with regret. It may not look like it or feel like it right now, but you will soon learn how all of the decisions you made molded you into the person you are today. I have learned that feeling my grief and leaning into it is the only way to get through such a painful experience.

After months of enduring this viscous divorce, we finally got to the day our divorce was supposed to be final. Throughout the process my husband or his attorney wouldn't submit requested documents. This would always delay the process. The day of the divorce we weren't able to finalize the divorce because my husband and his attorney had not submitted the list of items my husband wanted out of the house.

My attorney had requested this information months in advance. Turns out, on the day of the divorce, we couldn't agree on various items including the dog. They also didn't submit tax information, and we couldn't finalize the divorce without having these documents filed. The ultimate delay in my opinion was his inconsiderate and arrogant attorney. During the day of what was supposed to be the finalization of the divorce, his attorney left for 2 hours to go to another trial. I was in complete and utter shock. I even asked my attorney if I could send my husband's attorney my bill. We had to sit there, and wait for his attorney to finish with another case. By this time, it was the end of the day, and we had not come to an agreement. A few weeks later I received a notice in the mail that stated our court hearing was set for 5-6 months later for our divorce to be final.

One month after our divorce was supposed to have been finalized; we had to appear in criminal court for domestic violence. On this day, he was charged with criminal domestic violence. He was no longer permitted to have access to a firearm. He was ordered to be on probation, a fine, jail time if he violated the restraining order, and ordered to attend anger management classes. The judge told me he wished he could do more. He believed me, and stressed that I should have gone to the hospital right away. The judge stressed that I should have had him arrested each time the police came to the house. After my husband was sentenced, my husband turned in my direction, and had a smirk and smile on his face as if this entire situation was funny.

He loved to flex his dimples and let them show real deep after he had done something "dirty" or devious to someone. This is the same exact look he gave me. I was in complete shock once again by his behavior. I couldn't believe this became a joke to him.

I had always tried to be considerate of his colostomy bag. However, before I knew it, as he and his attorney walked by me I blurted out, "You still have that bag." The smile quickly left his face as a look of sadness came over him." For the first time, he looked shocked and maybe a little broken. I was surprised I said it, so I know he was even more surprised that I said something like that.

His attorney stopped right in front of me and stared at me. My legal advocate immediately told me, "Be quiet and keep your mouth shut. Go straight to the conference room and don't say a word. Don't even as much as look at him." I felt like child being scolded, but for the first time I felt like I had stood up for myself. It felt good. Once we got to the conference room, she explained to me that his attorney wanted a reason to charge me with contempt of court.

As my husband told me so many times that he studied me. He bragged about how he knew me better than I knew myself. I look back, and it pains me to see where he was right. He knew exactly what to do or say to hurt me, and that smirky smile cut and hurt me to the core.

Months prior to his death, I told my therapist how divorce feels so much worse than death. At the time, I thought at least with the grief of a death, the person is dead. It was painful to be physically abused by him, abused and humiliated through social media, and abused by him and his attorney during the divorce. It was just so much more painful to know the person is alive, and walking around and slandering you to anyone who will listen. As well as waging an evil hurtful smear campaign on multiple social media sites.

I was so hurt and broken the last time I came home from criminal court. I fell to the floor and asked God to comfort me. I didn't want Him to take away my pain because at this point I understood that I had to experience this pain for growth. I understood that I needed to turn my pain into power. I told God that I love my husband. I asked God why my husband would never see how much I loved him. I asked God why I was never good enough for my husband. Finally, I said God, "I release him to you. I can't love him enough. I can't prove my loyalty enough. I let go. God, He is yours."

I cried for hours after this. I even wrote it on my vision board that I was no longer going to hold on to the hope that my husband would be nice to me again, and on this day I let go. I let go of wishing things could go back to the way they used to be. I let go of thinking that he could have ever loved me. The ultimate emotional pain came 11 days later when I found out on a social media site that he passed away.

As I said before, no one contacted me to tell me he had collapsed or passed away. Not one of his family members, not the pastor or his wife, not his attorney, no one. Even if they cared nothing about me, our daughter is their flesh and blood and a minor child. I saw it on social media and began to make phone calls to find out the details. I called my attorney, and his attorney never contacted her to at least let our daughter know her father passed away. His parents sent his body directly from the hospital to the crematorium. Luckily I was able to track down the body. I spoke with the funeral director and made special arrangements to pay for our daughter to have a private viewing of her father. I felt she needed some sort of closure, even if it meant seeing her father for one last time with no answers. I was willing to pay what I needed in order to give her that closure. The funeral director relayed a message to me from my abuser's abusive attorney, that if my daughter and I showed up to the church for the service, he instructed my abuser's family to call the police and have me arrested.

I later found out that he collapsed at one of his many girlfriends' home. When I found out he passed away, the moment was surreal. I cried, I wept, and the pain was unreal. I felt a sense of relief and grief all in the same moment. I felt relieved knowing he could never physically harm me again, but I grieved for the loss of knowing I would never see him again. I grieved for our daughter knowing she could never rebuild a relationship with her father. I grieved for the finality of all of what could have been had he not crossed paths with the doctor who performed his surgery.

I was broken. At the time, I didn't think I could ever be mended. What I learned during this process is, you will be broken as long as you allow yourself to be broken. You will be broken if you don't take the time to love yourself first and rebuild your self-esteem. As your self-worth begins to blossom, all of the excruciating pain you are feeling will slowly fade away. You will begin to see your abuser for the abusive individual he is. You may even question your decision to leave, to file a police report, to file a protection order, to go to the hospital for an exam, to establish no contact with your abuser, or any other major decision.

You will question yourself only because of the deliberate action of your abuser to brainwash you, and reprogram your decision making thought process. You have been reprogrammed to second guess yourself as a result of tactics used by your abuser to lower your self-esteem, and diminish your self-confidence. You will have moments when you think you are missing your abuser. I can tell you right now. You don't miss your abuser; you miss the idea of the fictional character your abuser portrayed himself to be. You are grieving the devastation of your dreams, your marriage, relationship, unfulfilled plans, and the time you can never get back.

The pain and heartache you experienced during your relationship and marriage is no comparison to the emotional pain you will endure once you have separated from your abuser. So many people including myself were under the impression that if I just left my pain would end. My intent is not to scare you into staying, but I want to be transparent and honest when I tell you that once you leave your abuser, this is only the beginning of a very deep painful emotional journey back to who you are at the core.

You will most likely experience a wave of emotions. The emotions you feel will be both positive, and negative towards yourself and your abuser. This is a very crucial time where you really need to be kind to yourself, love yourself, be gentle with yourself, find your voice, build your strength, and hold on tightly to your faith. This is not an easy task especially when you have been told that you are worthless, or that no one will like you or love you.

My self-esteem and self-worth plummeted after I began to be physically abused. It was like an instant drain. I was suffering emotionally in the worst kind of way because I couldn't understand when or how I had lost myself. I wanted the old me back. I wanted the fire back that used to burn inside of me.

I made a non-negotiable decision with myself to be a better version of myself. I wanted to heal, and make a comeback of a more confident me, a fearless me, a woman who loved herself first, and a woman who had a mindset filled with the determination to create a new life of abundant possibilities. No matter how low or lonely you are feeling right now, I am here to tell you that you are loved, I believe in you, and you are more than enough. Your journey to healing won't be easy, but it will be worth it.

There were so many days when I would wake up and it was a struggle to get out of the bed. It was an even bigger struggle to face another day. I was thankful that God gave me the gift of having life to be able to wake up in the morning and see another day, but I would dread knowing I had to face another day not knowing what new dirty trick he and his attorney had up their sleeves. Sometimes I would just cry asking God to get me through because the pain was unbearable, and I would find myself curled up again in a fetal position asking God to comfort me.

The process of healing is so very important to your self-esteem, your self-worth, your self-confidence, and how you value yourself. Your emotional well-being and healing is a top priority. Just as our physical body gets sick and feels pain, so does your emotions. When our emotions get sick, we feel pain and discomfort, but we are less likely to do what is necessary to heal our emotions.

If we have a deep wound in our body, we will go to the doctor and seek medical treatment to heal that deep wound because the pain is hard to deal with. After feeling the pain and seeing the devastation of the deep wound in your body, you may become afraid of what caused that deep wound. It is hard to not think about the pain because it hurts so badly. This is what happens with the emotional abuse that your abuser inflicts upon you.

Have you ever noticed when you focus your mind on other things the pain of the wound does not hurt so much, and as time goes by the wound heals and the pain subsides. I wish this was not as difficult of a task when it comes to healing the wounds of domestic abuse and violence. Our hearts have been broken and we think about the pain and what caused our broken heart.

We seem to get stuck in a cycle of wanting to know why our abuser did what he did, or why we allowed it to happen. The list goes on. We feel stuck as if we can't move forward. We begin to live with the fear of when will it happen again, and this makes it challenging to move forward. If our self-esteem had not been so deeply damaged, and we had the support or resources we needed, some of us would run like hell and never look back.

Healing Process

Music is a very powerful healer. As a child and a teenager I listened to music all of the time, and I loved to sing. As a matter of fact, this is something my husband said he loved about me, and later he told me he always hated that I had such a beautiful voice. He said he wished he could sing half as good as I could. After that, because I didn't want to offend him, I stopped singing around him and ultimately stopped singing or listening to music altogether. It didn't take much because after my father passed away, I stopped singing publicly.

Now as I rebuild my life, self-confidence, self-esteem, and self-worth I listen to music. Music inspires me, encourages me, empowers me, uplifts me, and it makes me feel good. I won't listen to the songs we shared because it is too painful. However, I will listen to music that made me happy prior to meeting him and also new music that can't trigger a memory good or bad. It is unbelievable how good memories of him are just as painful as the bad memories. Why? Because the good memories will never happen again, and the thought of it all being built on a lie is a hard pill to swallow.

Healing From All of the Pain

When a woman loses her self-esteem she feels worthless. I gave so much of myself that I was stripped of my self-esteem when I allowed my life to be overtaken by my abuser. The process was so smooth and methodical that I allowed my abuser to come into my life and control me, manipulate me, and abuse me. I developed the disease to please based on how he would treat me if he didn't get his way. This was the formation of my disease to please in this relationship.

I felt like if I didn't go along with what he wanted and try to love him, heal him, and fix him; that I would be rejected, abandoned, unloved, disowned, and disliked. I was so caught up in pleasing my abuser that I risked my own life to make sure that he would give me the love that I thought I needed, or would remain by my side because I was loyal and faithful to him. I was so desperate to be loved that I accepted being lied to, lied on, beat, raped, abused, manipulated, cheated on, and degraded. I wanted to feel appreciated, and I accepted the bad behavior from someone whose only interest was in using me for what he and his parents could get from me.

This is what I thought I needed to take and endure to get what I thought was love only to get not even an ounce of love because it was not love. I ended up sacrificing myself and everything about me. I can't even say everything I stood for because I had never stood for anything not even standing up for myself. Even though I disagreed with so many of the things my abuser had said and done to me, I still remained with him because if I didn't go along with what he did, said, or wanted he would threaten to leave me.

My abuser frequently reminded me that he knew I would take his mess because he witnessed how much mistreatment I had taken from my own mother for so many years. This should have been an eye opener for me, but instead I made sure I didn't do anything to make him want to leave me or no longer love me. Once again, I ignored me in order to make sure I didn't lose his love. In an essence, I had lost my voice.

Sometimes we can resent our lives and hate our situations, but we have to take a step back and look at the cycle we are in. If we are not careful, we can create these situations because we don't want to deal with the pain of looking deep within ourselves. We have to resolve the painful issues of our past before running off to someone with the hope of them easing our pain. We have to stop doing what we hate. If you don't like that your father abused your mother, your mother abused you, or you are self-abusing with food or some kind of substance. Instead of jumping into a relationship with someone -- you have to work on yourself. Jump into an intimate relationship with yourself by doing the work on yourself to find out why these things happened, why you may or may not have allowed it to happen, how it make you feel, and why did it make you feel that way. Sometimes leaning into the pain is the only way to begin to heal. Healing yourself should be your number one priority. This will increase your self-esteem, self-worth, self-love, self-respect, and overall self-being. It will allow you to recognize toxic people and toxic behaviors.

It's all about breaking the chain, breaking the cycle. I wanted to give my daughter a two parent loving home and instead it was everything that I didn't want. Everything that I didn't want in a marriage is everything that I got. I didn't want a worldly man. I didn't want an abusive man, a cheater, liar, thief, lazy man, deceptive, yet those were all of the things that he brought to the table.

Breaking the chain and breaking the cycle is so important. I was so manipulated so much; I no longer knew my name. I knew I needed to make a change in my life when I started answering to "bitch." That's a problem especially when someone is being sarcastic and calling you "Dr. Bitch" to try and completely undermine your hard work and accomplishments. The bigger problem with this is that I answered to it for the sake of keeping peace. I stayed, and tried to understand why I would answer to something so degrading.

In order to heal from all of the pain and trauma, you have to use what you have been through as fuel to do something greater in life. You must be determined to succeed. Your will to survive and thrive must be greater than your abuser's mission to destroy you. When you are down to nothing and everyone you thought you could count on is nowhere to be found. You have no other choice but to keep moving forward towards a better way of life. You create your own story. Stop allowing others to be the star in your life.

Forgive Yourself

Maya Angelou says, "When you know better you do better." You didn't know, and it is safe to forgive yourself. During my search for knowing I mattered and rebuilding my worth I came across a woman named Louise Hay. I used her technique called "mirror work" to begin to embrace and love myself again.

Every morning when I get up, and every night before I go to bed I force myself to look at myself in the mirror and tell ME that I LOVE ME. Some days it is hard, but in order to heal and forgive myself I do it. It sometimes makes me sad to know that I neglected myself for someone who ultimately didn't love me. If this technique speaks to you, feel free to try it.

I am learning in every bad situation there is something good that will come out of it. I am thankful for being able to share this book and my journey with you. I am grateful that you have given me the opportunity to support you. I have heard various opinions from people on how they think I should heal. I believe within my heart that we all heal differently in our own time and way. I struggled for quite some time after the abuse to forgive myself, my abuser, and heal from the wounds of my past. At the time, I didn't realize how useful this would be, but it turned out to be extremely therapeutic. I was so brainwashed that even after I had been beaten and abused I would still act as though my husband could do no wrong. I was angry with myself that I couldn't seem to turn something on in my brain to be angry with him. I found myself angrier with myself when I should have been angry with him.

I sat down one day and I wrote a list of over 100 reasons why I no longer needed to be with my husband. The list could definitely go on, but I just needed enough reasons to make me realize I am worth more and deserve better than the degrading and abusive treatment from him and some of his family members. Sometimes I get caught up in only remembering the good times and think about the good times that could have been.

I had to write these things out on paper so I could see it. My mind would sometimes race, and I would block out how mean, crude, and nasty he would be to me. He was always very good at sweet talking me and reeling me back in when I would tell him I wanted out of the marriage or relationship prior to marriage. So many times we marry abusive men thinking their vile treatment towards us will get better. As some of you may or may not know: verbal, emotional, financial, sexual, and spiritual abuse is a prelude to physical abuse.

I didn't know this. The last time he put a knife to my throat and wanted to have a knife fight before I could leave, it still didn't resonate loud enough that I needed to leave before he eventually killed me. The scary part is that I would wake up in the middle of the night, and my heart would be pounding because I would think I was being choked by him again. For the first time in my life I didn't want to rewind time. I wanted to fast forward and skip the process of having to feel and endure such intense pain.

Self-forgiveness

Seeking self-forgiveness is a very important part of healing the emotional wounds of your past. We need to forgive ourselves so we can grow. Forgiving ourselves means admitting our shortcomings, and letting go of wishing we had done things differently to protect ourselves. Loving and forgiving yourself begins when you stop holding yourself accountable for the things someone else has done to you. You have been through some painful and hurtful experiences, and you have to forgive yourself. You can't hold yourself accountable for someone else's actions.

Along my journey of healing and self-discovery so many people stressed that I needed to forgive my abuser in order to let go and move on. The unbelievable part for me was that I still loved my abuser and it was so much easier to forgive my abuser than it was to forgive myself for being abused. Punishing yourself for the decisions you have made doesn't serve you.

Focus on being kind to yourself and loving yourself, so you ensure a future without abuse. When you hold yourself accountable for someone else's actions, you carry shame, guilt, and the weight of burdens that are not yours to carry. If you are caught in a cycle of questioning the decisions you made to keep you and your children safe, you are possibly preventing yourself from living a full life.

Self-forgiveness is one of the many ways that allows us to have peace of mind. Self-forgiveness is a priceless gift. It is a gift of restoration. Restoration is the act of being made whole again.

When you feel good about yourself again, the following things will happen in your life. You will:

- Get focused and stay focused
- Get motivated and stay motivated
- Set goals and pursue them
- Depend on yourself and be independent
- Not experience a high level of anxiety in the face of adversity
- Embrace ourselves for who we are
- See ourselves as lovable and capable
- Have a strong belief in ourselves
- Have a positive mindset and outlook on life
- Pursue a new career, education, or become an influencer in your field
- Feel more alive
- Have hope for a better future
- Attract healthy relationships that are not abusive
- Decrease your level of stress

- Become a social butterfly and interact with people
- Pay close attention to yourself and engage in self-care
- Have an open mind to new opportunities, and take risks to enhance your life
- Have the freedom to live life on your own terms
- Have a strong sense of boundaries and beliefs
- See improvements in your physical health
- Be able to spend time with your family and friends

Write down some things in your life that you need to forgive yourself for. Work on forgiving yourself and being kind to you.

Accepting that I didn't treat my ex husband great and there was some DV from me.

My rebellion as a teenager because I could of ended up dead

Not keeping myself 100% safe.

Believing I am unworthy of friendships because of what past friends have done.

Not being good at Mams

❖ Speak Up & Get Out! ❖

What's Really Inside of You?

Now that we have taken a look at your mindset and how you view life, it's time to take a look at your heart. Take the time to examine your heart. Yes, right now your heart is aching. But I want you to inspect your heart so you can heal your heart. Prepare yourself to accept what you discover, and be honest with your answers. What pain, hurt, betrayal, or discomfort has set up shop in your heart? For each of the things that you may be harboring in your heart, ask yourself the following questions:

Why are these feeling there?

failure, fear, Anxiety, Sadness

Does it help me?

Not all of the time Though, anxiety can challenge to do something.

Is it holding me back? If yes, How? Why?

Yes it is because I am isolated and lonely, and sometimes I fear being unable to maintain relationships with others.

How is it helping me?

I don't believe my situation is helping me. Anxiety will make me change a situation, if I can.

How is it holding me back?

My situation holds me back because I am alone and want to have a friendship.

What can I do to release it?

I really don't know.
☒ Work
☒ University.

As a heart and mind exercise ask yourself the following:

How much negative thinking do you do?

Most of the time.

Is your life going the way you want, need, or desire it to be?

In some ways yes but not all of it.

Believe it or not, there is a connection between your thoughts, what you carry in your heart, and the results you are seeing in your life. You can only go as far as your mind goes. If you have a limited mindset it will reflect in your life. People wonder why they keep getting the same old results. They get the same old results because they keep doing the same old self-sabotaging habits. Stop allowing negative thoughts to enter your mind and then reacting to those negative thoughts.

Some habits are extremely hard to break, and changing what and how you think is not an easy task. Self-sabotaging and self-destructive thoughts are even more difficult to transform. I will share some techniques and strategies you can implement immediately to lift yourself up out of the valley of despair. Remember, life is all about choices and it is up to you to choose whether or not you have positive or negative thoughts.

It's a lot easier to follow through on your decisions when you have made the right choice. Sometimes we question our decisions, but it is important to continue moving forward when we know we have done the right thing. If you have a plan, make up your mind ahead of time, and remain grounded in your values. You won't question them later on when tested. Yes, you will be tested. You are responsible for your safety and well-being. I have learned the hard way, no one else is your keeper.

Here are a few strategies that may help you in making the right choices and help you to avoid making bad decisions.

1. **Know who you are**. Know what negative thoughts you have and what gets you stuck in a rut. Is it the people you surround yourself with,

your environment, food, music etc…? Be very conscious of who you are at the core, what you stand for, and what triggers your negative thoughts.

2. **Surround yourself with healthy and positive people**. I can't stress this enough. You need to be around people who will genuinely love you, support you, and want the best for you. Not toxic people who want these things for you because of the benefits they will reap. I am talking genuine sincere people. Being surrounded by the wrong people will make your life much harder than it has to be.

3. **Get a Mentor**. Learn, learn, learn and keep learning. Seek people that have been through what you are going through. Take note of what they have done, or what they are doing and learn from them. Learn from people who have overcome the very thing you are struggling with. Take advantage of the wisdom and experience of those who have walked the path ahead of you. Coaches and mentors exist because they have been down the same or similar road and have triumphantly overcome the obstacles. They are willing to teach you and be there for those who are coming along behind them so you too can overcome your obstacles.

4. **Removing toxic people from your life is mandatory!** Yes, this is a very hard and painful thing to do. If you truly want to be free from abuse that is causing you pain or worse killing you. You must remove these people from your life. If you don't remove these people from your life, you must enforce the boundaries you create.

When you implement these changes in your life, you begin your journey to a happier and healthier life and mindset. If you are experiencing feelings of being overwhelmed, implement one strategy at a time. You will find that one strategy will lead to another. Live with intention and be proactive about your life and decisions. When you do, you will grow and see positive changes in your life.

❖ Speak Up & Get Out! ❖

What is your "I AM?" What positive words will you write and say after these two words to affirm YOU in a loving way every day?

I AM…

I Am *Caring*
I Am *Kind*
I Am *funny*
I Am *polite*
I Am *helpful*
I Am *supportive*
I Am *understanding*
I Am *loving*
I Am *encouraging*
I Am *forgiving*
I Am *quiet*
I Am *magintful*
I Am *worthy*
I Am *Intelligent*
I Am *Rebellious*
I Am _____
I Am _____
I Am _____
I Am _____
I Am _____
I Am _____
I Am _____
I Am _____
I Am _____

❖ Dr. Tamika Anderson ❖

Rebuilding Your Self Esteem

Your self-esteem plays an essential role in how you perceive yourself and contributes to your overall happiness and success in life. Your self-esteem is determined by how much you love yourself. The love you have for yourself is a reflection of how you perceive and value your self-worth. Ultimately, your self-worth will be your compass for developing and maintaining healthy relationships. Having a high level of self-worth and valuing your self-worth will enable you to enforce the boundaries you create and not allow abusive people to diminish who you are.

Your self-esteem is a vital part of your core being. It is very important to begin loving yourself again, forgiving yourself, and rebuilding your self-esteem and self-worth. It's okay to get to know who you are again. After all, you lost yourself by pouring your all into someone who didn't value your worth. On your path to healing it will take time, but you will find strength and when you do, hold on tightly to it.

On the journey of rebuilding your self-esteem, you are going to hurt as long as you allow yourself to hurt. I am not saying don't cry. You have to cry and feel the pain. It's a part of the healing process. You will hurt as long as your self-esteem is low. As you begin to do the work, and commit to doing things that will strengthen and empower you. Your pain will decrease, and you will see your abuser for exactly who and what he is. You will only question your decision to SPEAK Up and Get Out because you have been programmed to think he is always right and you are always wrong.

You don't miss him; you miss the person he pretended to be. You are mourning the destruction of hopes, dreams, and your marriage, relationship, and the time you invested in it. Find strength in knowing there is absolutely nothing to be ashamed of regarding what your abuser did to you. The general public continues to victim-blame, victim-shame, and ask the wrong questions when it comes to domestic violence and abuse. I overcame the shame and blame by speaking up and reaching out to professionals for help. My saving grace is being able to inspire, empower, and educate other women. The more I hear about women like me, the more I understand the abuse was not my fault. We don't have to carry the shame that our abuser should carry but never will.

As you begin to increase your self-esteem and value your worth, you will begin to believe in yourself, and your confidence will increase. The negative thoughts will eventually fade away and not be as constant. You will begin to trust yourself, your skills, and your decisions without second guessing. Your goal is to become self-assured and know that your life after abuse will be much better.

Get Comfortable with Being Alone with Yourself

As I was in the midst of trying to crawl my way out of this storm, I couldn't help but to think about the movie Ray. My mind drifted to the scene where Jamie Foxx who played Ray Charles was experiencing withdrawal. I felt like, and sometimes I feel like I was addicted to my husband. I feel like I am recovering from being addicted to a powerful drug that will hopefully someday leave my system. I take each day one day at a time.

After I left the last time and came back and then the final separation, I found myself always curled up in a ball crying uncontrollably. I was hurting because he was no longer living in our home. It was like I couldn't get him out of my system, and I still yearned for him even though I knew he was toxic to me and for me. I had to face the harsh reality that he was more of a habit than an added value to my life or a need in my life. Was I so broken that I was just going through the motions of having the comfort of knowing someone else was there? Was I so afraid of being on my own or feared being alone? I don't know.

Think about the following questions when it comes to addressing your own fears:

Could it be that we put more trust in our abusers, and depend more on them to take care of us? How can you trust yourself and depend on yourself?

Independence
Standing up and making decisions

Do you get caught up in the false sense of security with having your spouse or partner around even though he is abusive? How can you create security for yourself?

N/A

Could it be that we are afraid to depend on ourselves, and trust that we can take care of ourselves in a way that no one else can? How can you begin to take care of yourself in a way that no one else can?

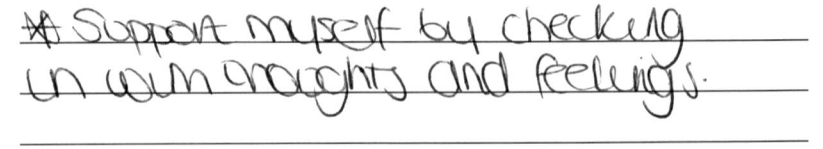

Support myself by checking in with thoughts and feelings.

These are just a few questions I ask myself in hopes of getting stronger, wiser, and more courageous each day. What is my level of:

- Self Love
- Self Worth (Know your worth and value who you are)
- Self Esteem
- Self Respect
- Spiritual development (meditation, affirmation, positive mindset)
- Healing from all of the pain

CHAPTER 11

Thrive and Fly

"Our first and last love is self love." ~Christian Nestell Bovee

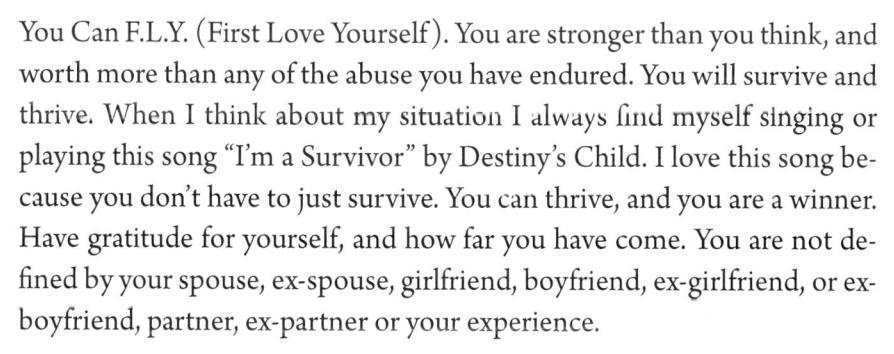

―― ∽ ――

You Can F.L.Y. (First Love Yourself). You are stronger than you think, and worth more than any of the abuse you have endured. You will survive and thrive. When I think about my situation I always find myself singing or playing this song "I'm a Survivor" by Destiny's Child. I love this song because you don't have to just survive. You can thrive, and you are a winner. Have gratitude for yourself, and how far you have come. You are not defined by your spouse, ex-spouse, girlfriend, boyfriend, ex-girlfriend, or ex-boyfriend, partner, ex-partner or your experience.

You will begin to realize how your abuser taught you valuable lessons about yourself. Forgiving him and forgiving yourself are very important components on your journey of healing. Releasing resentments is for your well-being, not his. You can do whatever you want. Go for your dreams. Achieve your goals. You are loved. You are confident. You are powerful. You are beautiful inside and out.

Don't focus on what others say about you, or what they are doing. Focus on you, your children, your spirituality, your happiness, and your relationship with your higher power. Be happy with living your life. Live for you. Know your worth and pursue your dreams. Life is a gift. Enjoy the blessing of life and expect new miracles, and strive to be better today than you were yesterday.

❖ Dr. Tamika Anderson ❖

Letting Go of Negative Thinking

Your mindset is everything when it comes to how you view yourself. When you are living with a negative mindset you won't be able to live a successful and confident life. If you are living with a negative mindset all of your efforts to do anything will be very hard to achieve. A negative mindset will cause every aspect of your life to be unstable. Negative thinking will distort your perception of the gifts, talents, and abilities you have been blessed with. The affects negative thinking can have on you can cause you to miss opportunities, and keep you from living in your truth and purpose. The way you think about things or view situations contribute to the choices you make in your life.

A negative mindset is toxic. A toxic mindset can consume you. If you have been following me, you know I talk a lot about taking the Weeds and Seeds Inventory. Take a look at all of the people around you. Are they positive or negative? Do they genuinely support you, or do they not support you? Extremely negative people can affect you in a way that their negative energy can cause you to be negative. These weeds can squeeze the life out of you. When you determine who the weeds are in your life, it is important to put an end to these relationships. Once you have transformed your mindset and removed the toxic people out of your life, you can begin to live a successful life and be of service to others. Remember change is a painful process.

I like to read this really old book, and in this old book it talks about reaping what you've sown. If we do good things, good things will come back to us, and if we do bad things, bad things will come back to us. For some, this is also known as Karma. We shouldn't focus on seeking revenge because the bad things that someone does to us will come back to them. They will suffer the consequences.

Full forgiveness can take time. In order for forgiveness to be effective, it is important to be sincere and straight from the heart. One technique in the process of forgiveness is to remember what was done to you, but letting go of the pain associated with it. Remember, forgiveness is not about benefitting your abuser, but more about releasing you from the past.

There are two traps that I fell into. I was frustrated and humiliated for years because my abuser lied all of the time and manipulated so many situations. He liked to play mind games by lying, and then throwing hints that he was lying. He seemed to enjoy me begging him to just be honest with me. I was angry and held a grudge because these interactions were exhausting, and kept me on a confusing emotional roller coaster. It was like being on an unending merry-go-round that I couldn't get off of. I was angry because he would lie, and laugh about his lies. The high level of arrogance was grossly indescribable.

Coping with Anger

After my abuser starting physically abusing me, I was flooded with anger. I was angry with myself for allowing him, my mother, and others to walk all over me like a doormat. I was angry that I never had the courage to stand up for myself. I was angry that they were able to turn people against me with lies. I was angry that my mother never allowed me to have a voice, and then I married a man who did the same. I was angry that I had loved him unconditionally throughout the years, and I had put up with his lying, cheating, bad behavior, and even rude behavior from some of his family members.

I was angry with my mother because if she would have loved me the way I should have been loved as a child, I wouldn't have been searching for love in all of the wrong places. I was angry with my mother and sister for allowing my sister's Indonesian boyfriend to molest me, and sexually violate me at 9 years old. I was angry that I confided in my abuser about my molestation and he laughed and told me I probably liked it. I was angry that my father died, and left me behind to have to continue dealing with my mother's abusive behavior. I was so focused on getting as far away from my mother, and not ever being good enough in her eyes that I married her in the form of my husband.

I was angry that the 2 people who were supposed to love, nurture, and protect me were the ones who treated me the worst in life. I was angry that they both were controlling, possessive, and critical of everything I did. I was angry that no matter how much I gave of myself, love, time, or money it was never good enough for them. I had to gradually learn to let go of the anger I was holding onto, and use it as fuel to rebuild my life.

Anger is a natural human emotion that can also be a powerful motivating force. Anger can be healthy and beneficial under certain circumstances. It is okay to get angry. Expressing anger is okay as long as you are not hurting yourself or others. However, getting angry and staying angry is not healthy. Staying angry with yourself or someone else is counterproductive and self destructive. Anger can cause all sorts of health issues.

You won't grow stewing in a pool of anger. You will remain where you are, and nothing in you or around you will change except the rising level of your anger. When someone makes you mad, use that emotion of anger, and focus the energy into changing your situation for the better. If you feel like there is nothing you can do to change your situation, do something for yourself, and be kind to yourself until you can change your situation. Whatever you do, don't allow anger to keep you rooted in your problems.

Letting Go of Grudges

We all have at least one person we can think of that we have vowed to never speak to again for as long as they live. You may even have several people that you can think of because many times abusers will allow other people to abuse you. You may have grown to resent the people who have abused you. Don't allow this resentment to turn into bitterness. Your feelings of anger and resentment can turn into bitterness. This bitterness can cause you to hold a grudge. For some people holding a grudge has become second nature. Holding grudges holds you captive to the person or situation you are hurt, bitter, or angry about. It's easy to form a grudge because your pain tells you it is justified. However, once the grudge is formed it is very hard to let it go.

It is very important to let go of grudges, so you can have and maintain a positive attitude. Holding a grudge is fertile ground for a negative attitude. Having a negative mindset for a significant length of time will poison your mental garden. This negative mindset will constantly remind you of all of the negative people or experiences in your life.

By feeding a grudge, you are using energy that can be used to strengthen and enrich you own life. If you choose not to interact with the people who have hurt you, that is a decision you can make. You have to protect yourself. More importantly, if you choose to go your separate ways, letting go of what was said or done to you makes you a better person on the inside and outside. You release the power someone has over you by letting go of the pain and hurt of their actions.

Forgive Yourself

Be kind and gentle to yourself. You did the very best that you knew how at the time. You believed and trusted your abuser and you got conned. You are not alone. You may not feel like it right now, but you do have a life and you will move forward with your life. The memories of the abuse I think will always stay with us, but overtime those memories will become a distant memory. I still deal with the guilt of allowing someone to control me, and having my life revolve around someone else. It is time to forgive yourself and take your life back.

Freeing yourself by Forgiving Others

One of the most difficult things to do after someone has abused you is to forgive them for what they have done. Forgiving someone who has wronged you is vital. When we hold on to the things they have done to us it keeps us at the same level as them. It holds us in bondage. Holding on to the hurt and pain will affect you mentally, emotionally, physically, spiritually, and even financially.

Letting go of all of these things will give you a new perspective on life. Forgiving your abuser allows you the opportunity to have a clear understanding of what forgiveness really means and how freeing it can be. Forgiveness is also an act of compassion and empathy. It is easy to harbor feelings of not wanting to forgive. It's easy to be bitter and carry hatred in our hearts.

It's also easy to get caught in the cycle of replaying in our minds over and over again the negative things that have been done to us. Sometimes the only thing you can think of is how bad you were hurt or wanting to seek revenge on the person or people who hurt you. I say people because 9 times out of 10 you were or are with your abuser because you experienced abuse by someone else at a younger age. You ultimately gravitated toward what was familiar.

Love Yourself

I stress this all of the time. You must love yourself. Why, because you truly deserve it. Your abuser's goal is to break you down in any form possible. I know I still have days where I want to throw in the towel and my abuser is no longer alive. Somehow that still small voice speaks to me and wakens my spirit to keep fighting.

They have tried to destroy you piece by piece. You have to dig deep to put yourself back together. This time around, they won't be in control. You will be in control of living a fulfilled life. You will rebuild your self-confidence, self-esteem, and become your authentic self. You will grow and bloom into a beautiful and very strong woman. Be unapologetically you!

One of the exercises that really helped me was to write down everything I love about myself. I understand some of you may still be with your abuser. But for those of you who are able to do this, write down what you love about yourself. Then cut them out and post them around your home, on your wall, or where you can see them. I posted mine on my bathroom mirror and wall. I also posted on the wall at the foot of my bed, so each morning when I woke up the first thing I saw was something positive about me. Seeing or reading something positive about yourself can be very cathartic as well as encouraging.

No matter what type of abuse you have experienced, the time during and after the trauma of the abuse is a very difficult, lonely, and a delicate time. You have most likely been isolated by your abuser from your family and friends. Don't let shame and guilt keep you from reaching out to build or rebuild a trusted circle of people who will support you in some capacity.

This trusted circle of people can be an outlet for you to share your troubles and concerns. You may find this circle to be very small. That's okay as long as they can give you words of encouragement to keep you going and focused. It's always good to have support, so you can maintain a high level of hope even when the bend in your tunnel prevents you from seeing the light at the end.

Some of you may be in a position where you have no one to turn to. This was a very painful reality for me. I learned about different types of people during this time. There were those who came in the name of help but stole from me. Those who came in the name of help and tried to manipulate, and use me because they saw me as weak. They thought there was an opportunity to take advantage of me. Then you have the people who will contact you in the name of concern or prayer and as soon as you share your story with them you don't hear from them again. These are the people who want to get your business and use it as a gossip conversation piece. They have no good intentions at all.

There are also the so called friends who seem to delight in your misfortune. These people are not your friends. They are toxic and you don't need to continue a relationship with them.

I found myself in this situation. I had to depend on me. I turned to God, books, the National Domestic Violence Hotline, and support groups. This is a great opportunity for you to begin to trust yourself again. Trust yourself enough to know you can get through such a painful and difficult time with or without support from others.

Keep a journal and detail your feelings, emotions, dreams, and desires. Write down your vision, and hold yourself accountable to moving forward and healing. Keeping a journal is very important. When you find yourself feeling discouraged and dejected, read your journal, and reflect on the things you have accomplished. Don't lose faith that your situation will change in your favor. In the midst of my storm, I posted notes all over the walls of my home.

My most favorite note to myself read, "In God's time, my situation will turn in my favor. Thank you God." You may want to write yourself notes of encouragement, and post them on your wall. So you can see them as soon as you wake up in the morning, or post them on your mirror. You can also set a reminder on your phone to remind you of something positive.

I mentioned earlier about doing a weeds and seeds inventory. Pay attention to what is growing in your mind and in your life. It may be very difficult some days, but you may have to be your own bucket of water and pour into yourself. Don't be afraid to water your worth and encourage yourself. Through your process of healing, you will become stronger and discover you have a green thumb for harvesting a new life free of abuse.

Your tender roots will grow into a strong sturdy tree. You will be able to weather some of the worst storms life may send your way. What you are going through is preparation for something greater in your life. You have to remain strong, and believe the blossoms of your determination will rise from the soil of the old you and bloom like a beautiful flower in the spring time.

CHAPTER 12

Closing Thoughts

"Birds sing after a storm; why shouldn't people feel as free to delight in whatever sunlight remains to them?" ~Rose Kennedy

---

During this painful journey, I came to realize that I had to get to know, love, nurture, heal, understand, and commit to me. I had to separate myself as a wife, mother, daughter, daughter-in-law, and all of the other titles I had been placed in a box and labeled with. I had to get to the core of who I was. I needed to peel back all of the onion layers of all of my past hurt, pain, grief, wounds, rejections, fears, and everything that held me back from speaking up for myself. I wanted to uncover what allowed me to allow someone to use me and abuse me. I needed to create a strong sense of who I am.

I had been stripped of who I thought I was, and as a result I bought into the things that were said about me. I spent too many years dimming my light for someone who had an issue with who I was and my accomplishments. My healing began when I decided to embrace who I am, flaws and all. I stopped trying to cover up the hurt and the pain. I decided to face those experiences head on and feel the pain. I leaned into the pain.

I wanted to finally feel the pain because I never want to feel anything like this kind of painful pain again in life. Feeling the pain and processing the pain has allowed me to empathize with others, and have deep compassion for them without feeling like I have to "fix" their problem. I now share with them how they too can take responsibility for themselves and implement various resources to grow through the process of their painful journey.

At some point in our life we began to accept abuse as a way of life to avoid the possibility of living life alone. We have accepted the instability that comes with being on an emotional roller coaster of toxic love. It doesn't have to always be this way. As you begin to rebuild your emotional muscle, and separate your emotions from your abuser. Your outlook on life and your survival will be completely different.

Yes, being on your own can be scary, and you may be fearful of the unknown. Once you breakthrough your fear you will gain independence, and experience the freedom of an abuse free life. Taking the time to get to know who you are again will bring stability back to your life. You will be able to have firm boundaries that won't allow you to settle for less than what you are worth.

I have learned to honor who I am. I no longer compromise my morals, values, or beliefs for anyone. Not even in the name of love. My courage, strength, and knowing who I am won't allow me to lower my standards. I no longer care about what someone thinks about me, or what they say about me. I also realized that I was so eager to fix, nurture, and heal the pain of my abuser because I was too busy trying to run from my own pain, and grief from how my mother treated and still treats me.

I no longer have a fear of being alone. I no longer have the fear of not being able to make it on my own and be independent. I finally dusted off my wings, so I can take flight. My abuser's mother always told him not to trust me, and that I couldn't be trusted. This was a very painful experience. I never gave her a reason to say, or think I couldn't be trusted.

I lost myself in trying to please my abuser by trying to prove to him that I was trustworthy and loyal to him. I was on such a quest to prove myself that I no longer had boundaries and fell deeply into the people pleasing trap.

Know Your Worth

In order to avoid seeking affirmation just for the sake of being affirmed by someone else, you have to know your own worth. You have to have a set of beliefs, and standards that you stand firm on. I can't stress how important it is to be aware of what you believe in. When you are aware of what you believe in, you will have the confidence to voice your opinions, and follow the right path for yourself even when everyone else is against you.

Developing a healthy formula for knowing your worth will allow you to stand in your truth with fearless faith. As a reminder of the precious value of your worth, write down all of your good qualities to help guide you with increasing and maintaining a healthy level of confidence. Think about the issues that are important to you. This could be your family values, your career, your political views, or voicing your opinions/beliefs. These things should be a part of your worth code or formula.

Let what you value and stand for guide your actions in every situation. You should never violate your beliefs, or lower your standards to gain the approval of someone else. Take control of your life by having a voice and standing up for what you believe in. The moment you stop seeking validation from people who are toxic, you will grow much stronger. The people who are supposed to be in your life will love you, and embrace you for being who you are at the core. When you stand firm to these principles, you will have a greater sense of self. You will have so much self-confidence you won't want to second guess yourself or seek someone else's opinion.

If you find yourself going out of your way for others, bending over backwards trying to please them, and you are not getting anywhere - you need to remember to seek the most important things in life. Seek your High Power, God, Source, or the Universe first. Once you do this, everything will begin to line up in your life. Another mistake we make is thinking more highly of someone else instead of our Higher Power.

There is no one on this earth that can do for us what God can do for you. No one can heal your pain, fix your problems, or bring you inner peace. By constantly pleasing my abuser, I unknowingly made him an idol. I put him before God. I revered him. No one can replace God. When we knowingly or unknowingly do this, we will be sorely disappointed. When we put God first he will give us a fulfilled life, continue to love us unconditionally, and bless us abundantly.

I had to tell myself that there is a purpose and plan for my pain. I decided I was going to praise God through the pain, and praise him through the process. I learned to trust the plans that God has for my life. I would beg God to take away my pain until I realized I needed to embrace the pain. The deep dark emotional pain allowed me to grow, and it shifted my perspective. Embracing my emotional pain made me stop feeling sorry for myself. I had to understand that I was better off not being with him.

Once I fully grasped this, I went on a mission to fix me. I went on a mission to do some deep soul searching so I can be my authentic self. I had to shift my focus from wanting to be there for my abuser and helping him through all of his "stuff" to making sure I was taking care of me. That is something I didn't do throughout our relationship. I didn't take care of me.

Focus on the present. Take your mind off of what happened and what was. Looking back does not serve you. Practice controlling your thoughts. Focus on positive things in your life. Be grateful for how far you have come. Don't focus on what you have lost, or what you could lose. The most important thing right now is to focus on the present moment. Be present in the now. If not, anxiety will set in and set you back.

So many days I would dig really deep within myself trying to push through the pain of why this had to happen to me. I wondered why my life had been turned upside down. Why did I feel like I was in a blender being shaken and stirred? I had to just lean into my pain and finally stop resisting what I was feeling.

I now realize I am not alone, and I am not the only woman this has happened to. When it first happened I thought there were only a few women out there going through domestic abuse and violence. When I started trying to understand what domestic abuse is, and why men physically harm their spouse/partner. I was shocked by the staggering statistics.

I read something that said a stranger on the street will and can get more jail time for assaulting/abusing someone they don't know as opposed to a husband or boyfriend who only gets a slap on the wrist for abusing his wife, girlfriend, someone he knows, supposedly loves, or should be protecting. Connect with me on social media, or email me to share your thoughts about the book and the following questions.

My Questions to You Are:

Do you think there should be tougher laws and consequences for domestic violence or abuse?

If so, do you think there would be a decrease in the number of reported cases of domestic violence?

Do you think there would be a decrease in the acts of reported domestic violence cases?

Do you think tougher laws or consequences would put the victim in more danger or make her hesitant to report the crime because of the tough law against domestic violence?

Since domestic violence affects so many women and children, why haven't there been any tougher laws to legally punish these men for their brutal acts? I don't want this to be my dirty little secret any longer especially if it can save someone's life.

We all need that someone that makes us realize we are not alone. We need that affirmation to know that what we are feeling is valid and warranted. It takes some of us a little longer to learn how to break the cycle of domestic violence and abuse to take our life back into our own hands and gain control again. I believe that courage comes with time. It is our survival mechanism.

Verbal, physical, social media, emotional, sexual, spiritual, and financial abuse has no regard for may become a victim of domestic abuse and violence. Women from all races, age groups, income levels, religions, and educational backgrounds have fallen for the deceit of charming abusive men.

We are taught to believe that when someone tells us that they love us, we assume that love comes with respect, protection, compassion, and kindness. Unfortunately, this assumption positions us to learn, at some point during the relationship, that the person we have fallen so deeply in love with is only a wolf in sheep clothing.

I challenge you to never keep silent! Never doubt yourself! Never lower your standards! Never compromise your self-worth for anyone! Never doubt your intelligence, your God-given gifts, and your ability to have the strength and courage to stand up and save yourself. Just because you have a loving heart does not mean that you are not smart because you loved someone, and they took advantage of you kindness.

Don't continue to punish yourself because someone else made a reckless decision to mistreat you. Contrary to what you have been told, your being abused is **not** your fault. Be kind to yourself and be thankful that you are making the decision, or made the decision to Speak Up and Get Out!

I hope this book has been a source of healing for you. We take responsibility for our faults while understanding we are only human. We have a great capacity to forgive our abuser, and that compassion will eventually if not already apply to you. We don't hate all men. We don't even hate our abuser forever, and instead we transition from the hate we may have once felt into a state of healing.

When we learn to be honest and open with ourselves we are able to grow stronger. This book was written for women of domestic violence and abuse to gain strength from one another without taking another woman's strength. I want you to know that I love you and no matter what stage of healing you are in: you are valuable, you matter, and you are good enough.

About the Author

Dr. Tamika Anderson is an International best-selling Author, Speaker, Mentor, and Founder of the Speak up & Get out Movement. Dr. Tamika is a survivor of 20 years of Domestic Violence and Abuse. Inspired by her own Domestic Violence experience, Dr. Tamika's work aims to empower women and survivors of domestic violence through speaking, coaching, and mentoring. Dr. Tamika's dedication to helping women inspired her to write Speak Up & Get Out: A Guide to Survive & Thrive from the Devastation of Domestic Violence, an urgently needed and insightful guidebook for women to help them know the red flags of domestic violence and how to escape a potentially deadly relationship. Her book can also help supportive family members and friends better understand the dynamics of Domestic Violence.

Dr. Tamika knows from both personal experience and from experience in the trenches with victims and survivors of Domestic Violence that the trauma these women face are both terrifying and universal. Dr. Tamika's goal is to equip women with the tools and strategies they need to overcome their obstacles and live a life free from abuse.

Dr. Tamika holds a Bachelor of Arts in Psychology, a Master of Science in Organizational Leadership, a Doctor of Science in Information Systems & Communications and she is also a Certified Financial Manager through the United States Department of Defense. Dr. Tamika has also been featured on NBC, ABC, HLN, and FOX to spread her compelling message of Domestic Violence Awareness.

Connect With Me!

Website: www.TamikaAnderson.com

Email: SpeakUp@TamikaAnderson.com

Facebook: www.Facebook.com/ConneXtionWorks.com

Twitter: @ConneXtionWorks

Instagram: @DrTamikaAnderson

Youtube: ConneXtion Works

Resources

National Domestic Violence Hotline 1-800-799- SAFE (7233) / 1-800-787-3224 (TTY)

National Suicide Prevention Lifeline 1-800-273-TALK(8255)

Suicidepreventionlifeline.org

Thehotline.org

Womenslaw.org

Printed in Great Britain
by Amazon